Moose
The Story of a Very Special Person

by W. Scott MacDonald
and Chester W. Oden, Jr.

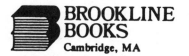
BROOKLINE BOOKS
Cambridge, MA

ACKNOWLEDGMENTS

Our appreciation and thanks to Joe Oden for use of his photos of Moose at age eighteen and for the cover photo, to Jan Webber and Barbara Armstrong for their valuable contribution in reviewing and editing the manuscript.

Second Printing:
W. Scott MacDonald, Ph.D., P.A.
21 Century Dr.
St. Paul, MN 55119

ISBN: 0-03-043936-1
Library of Congress Catalog Card Number: 78-50413

To those like Moose
and to those Moose loves

PREFACE

So often in the past, we have ignored the potential of a group of people we label "the handicapped." By ignoring their potential, we lessen our own.

This phenomena can be vividly seen in the life of Moose. Moose was welcomed into a loving family who resisted the advice of others to place him in an institution for the mentally retarded. Nevertheless, in their concern for his well-being, they expected too little of him.

Taught by society that a Down's syndrome child was helpless, Moose's parents raised him without challenging him to develop new skills and new ways of reaching out to others. But Moose's own inventiveness and his parents' willingness to learn from him enriched the life not only of Moose and his family but of all those who encountered Moose's specialness.

Our own family has known the enrichment that a child who is "different" can bring. We welcome with enthusiasm a book such as *Moose* which, in very human terms, teaches us that each of us is different and that we have our own unique capacity for loving, sharing, enjoying, and learning. I hope that you will find the same sense of wonder and delight that Hubert and I experienced in getting to know Moose through his story and in watching him grow to manhood.

We must open our hearts and minds to all people like Moose. They have much to teach us. If we allow them to share their uniqueness with us, all of us will be better able to achieve our potential as human beings.

Senator Muriel Humphrey
June 1978

CHAPTER ONE

As I sit here at the dining room table, savoring the last drops of my morning coffee, I watch Moose trot down the quarter-mile driveway to the bus stop. Seeing him go fills me with a joy that is hard to describe, even to myself. I find myself shaking my head, knowing I never expected to see this day.

I wonder what's happening in Moose's heart as he leaves expectantly for work? He knows people are counting on him to pull his weight, to make a contribution. And he must be terribly proud of himself, of being a genuine part of something, of being treated like everyone else. But there I go again. I've never heard Moose talk about pride. This is no time for me to put onto Moose the things I think should be there.

He's more a part of the family now than ever before, because he's part of the world of work. That seems to mean a lot to ol' Moose, and I'm happy with that.

I'm not saying the struggle is over. Some people will over-react to his problems; others will pretend they don't exist. So he'll have his share of hassles out there.

I wonder if he'll lose his bus coupon. He's still vulnerable in so many ways.

But today we're happy for him. We're hopeful. For an instant I close my eyes and remember how it all started.

* * *

Seems like yesterday I raced through the halls of the hospital to the maternity ward, barely beating the stork. I watched as the doctor and his coterie of interns fussed over my son for a moment and then gave him to Polly. Without waiting for the doctor's advice, she brought the child to her breast. She was radiant and proud.

"He's a beautiful, healthy baby, Chester," she said, seeing me.

We named him Chester Wayne Oden III.

Wayne looked so tiny I could hardly believe he weighed over ten pounds. The top of his head was slightly enlarged, but I knew from my medical school training that this was not uncommon. "Caput edema," I assured Polly. "It'll be normal in a few days."

But I didn't tell Polly what alarmed me. I couldn't put my finger on it, but I knew there was something wrong with our child. Polly had said Wayne was a healthy baby, and I figured she should know what she was talking about; after all, she'd had three children in a previous marriage, and Earl, Terry, and Mila were all beautiful, healthy kids. But I was worried nonetheless.

"He sucks strongly," Polly said, "and he has a good appetite."

I wondered if I was way ahead of myself, playing the doctor role. Was I prematurely diagnosing my son just to blow up my own sense of importance and intelligence? Maybe. But doubt crowded my guts and I'd learned not to ignore that feeling. I'd had it before; once in the 555th Airborne when we were testing experimental parachutes. I tried everything to get out of jumping that day, and finally, giving in to my intuition, I fell to the floor, doubled up with vicious stomach cramps. They scratched me that flight. Later, I checked my chute and discovered my gut feeling had saved my life. With a severely worn static line, I'd have bounced off the ground at 180 miles an hour, the chute still neatly folded on my back.

Now I had that same feeling about my son, Wayne.

When the nurse came to take Wayne to the nursery, I went with her. Though it was late at night, the nursery was lit up like a Christmas tree, and some babies were hollering at the tops of their lungs. I could see why—I'd holler too, if I had bright lights beating down on me twenty-four hours a day. I watched a nurse move to one of the babies and flick the bottoms of his feet, waking him so he could be fed. I asked the head nurse not to do that to Wayne and let the staff know I thought they should respond to the needs of the flesh rather than the convenience of the hospital.

When I returned to Polly, we had a long talk about ourselves and our family. The conversation was dizzying. Wayne was our fourth child; he would balance out the two girls and one boy we already had. We laughed about Earl, the oldest, and how he was already directing the activities of the two younger girls, determined to take over the roost. He read to them and worked hard to interpret the adult world to them as only an eleven year old can. Earl was an adult in so many ways: His interests were in books and serious study. In fact, he was a bit too serious for a child. But this was Earl.

Mila, our next child, was worldly, extremely bright, and fastidious. Hers was a practical intelligence: She could fix the things Earl would leave for broken, and she learned to cook like a pro, whereas Earl would satisfy himself with a spoonful of peanut butter. She patched up Earl's bruises, bandaged his sores, and easily remembered every item on a shopping list. I would ask Mila to look up technical words I ran across in my reading.

Then there was Terry. She had more sensitivity and raw talent than either of the others. She was as fine a student as her brother, though her scholarship tended toward the arts. She was absorbed in graphic arts and was highly skilled with oils.

And now Wayne—our fourth child and my first natural son. Another healthy child. . . .

Doctor Anderson hadn't said anything was wrong with Wayne, but the feeling in my stomach persisted, and somehow I had to respond to it. When I visited Wayne the next day, I donned a clean lab coat and went to the nursery, telling the charge nurse I was to do a "CBC," a complete blood chemistry, on the Oden baby. I quickly unwrapped a syringe, dabbed Wayne's head with alcohol, and slipped a needle into his throbbing anterior fontenal, the soft spot above his forehead. I extracted exactly one cc of blood and swabbed the tiny red dot before charging off to the lab. If Wayne's docs weren't going to tell me what the story was with my child, I'd have to discover it myself.

In the lab, I knew immediately from my work in hematology that the condition I found was not desirable in adults. In one frantic motion, I snatched a phone and a medical text. While I dialed Dr. Anderson, I located the section on infant hematology.

"This is Doctor Anderson." As Dr. Anderson's bright voice came over the phone, my finger ran over the description of normal infant's blood. Relief flooded me. The description matched Wayne's condition!

"Good morning, sir," I said, slightly embarrassed now. "I . . . just wanted to thank you for delivering Wayne."

"Not at all." He waited for me to carry the conversation.

"By the way," I added, trying to cover up my mistake, "I meant to ask about the caput edema."

Anderson sighed into the phone. "Oh, that," he began. I heard uneasiness in his voice, and the tight feeling returned, choking me so I couldn't speak.

"Don't worry about *that*," continued Dr. Anderson, cautiously. "It's normal . . . it'll disappear in a few days."

I could hear him pausing, picking out his next words.

"Chet," he began, "there's something else." Again he groped for words, "I'm only an obstetrician and. . . ." He cleared his throat, nervously. "Well, I called in another doctor. You may know him. Dr. Hampster."

"My God," I blurted, "what'd *he* say?"

"I think you should call him," Anderson said. "I'll talk to you later."

After he hung up I wanted to call him back, but hesitated. I dialed anyway. Busy. I dialed again. Busy. I swore that if I ever got that damned medical degree I'd take enough time to tell a person what the situation was. I'd never leave patients hanging by their imagination. I'd never consciously leave a man to worry about his twenty-six-hour-old son, to wonder what in the world warranted the consultation of an internationally-known pediatrician.

I had to get up and walk around the room. I stopped in front of a metal locker and stared at it, feeling hot tears of frustration in my eyes. I wanted to scream, "Doesn't anybody here care about my son? Don't my feelings count here?" But I didn't scream. I lashed out, slamming my fist against the locker. The door popped open and a purse fell out just as a nurse came up behind me, clucking her tongue at my outburst. I put the purse back and tried to close the door, but it was badly sprung and kept swinging open.

"I was thinking of my doctor," I said in explanation and turned on my heel. After three steps I stopped without turning around. "Send the bill to Chester Wayne Oden," I said. "Either of them."

By the time I got to my lab, I'd gotten hold of myself. Why get mad at Doc Anderson? He just did what he could. I remembered that I had to call Dr. What's-his-name and for an instant I looked around for another locker. But no, I had to find out about Wayne. This time I swallowed my feelings and dialed the phone.

"This is Chet Oden. Dr. Hampster has examined my child, and I'd like to talk to him."

"Dr. Hampster is with a patient now. He'll call you when he's available." The receptionist was about to hang up.

"Hey, wait," I said. "This is *Doctor* Oden, and Dr. Anderson said I should call. It's about my son." Bullshit! They'd skin me alive if they caught me, but I'd have done anything for some straight answers.

"I see," she said, acknowledging my name dropping. "I'll tell Dr. Hampster you called."

I didn't expect any special treatment, but dammit, there was something haywire with my newly born son, and no one seemed to care. Everyone knew that Dr. Hampster was only called in when things were serious, and yet his office was playing games with me.

I was glad to be alone, surrounded by sterile glass and stainless steel, where no one would intrude on my thoughts. I wondered if Hampster was not cloistered in some little office painted harsh white, poring over a pile of print-outs, trying to make the data conform to a pet theory of his while I and perhaps a dozen other parents tried to piece together the meager information we had about our newborn children. I wanted to know the facts. If Wayne had some condition that needed the attention of a doctor, then I wanted him to have it now. At the same time, I longed for the reassurance that Wayne was all right, that he would have my strong body and quick reflexes, that he would have at least the same chances I'd had to enjoy the world.

I drank some coffee and stared at the phone. The "In" tray was overflowing with tests to be run, and I absently picked up a test tube. Without looking at the name on the request, I automatically began running the test. I adjusted the focus on the microscope, suddenly disturbed because I realized I was running the test, not to relieve the anxieties of some unknown person, but to occupy *my* mind, to complete *my* assigned lab work. Damn, I thought. I'm like the rest of them.

Two days later, I was called to the phone.

"Dr. Oden," I heard Dr. Hampster say in a flat, disinterested tone. "My secretary said you called."

"Mister Oden," I corrected him. "Thanks for getting back. You saw my son, Wayne, at Dr. Anderson's request."

"Oh, yes." A glimmer of recognition. But still the flat, emotionless tone in his voice, as if he were sorting nuts and bolts. "Yes, Wayne Oden." Pause. "Your son already displays eight classic signs of Down's syndrome. I thought you might have seen it yourself, being in medicine."

"Down's syndrome?" My mind leafed through the medical diagnosis books, trying to grab onto the only real information I'd had about Wayne since his birth.

"Mongoloid," Dr. Hampster said. "People used to refer to children with Down's syndrome as mongoloids." Hampster went on as if he were lecturing to a class. "Your son will probably never walk or talk. He'll never be socialized, of course. Dr. Marquard in my department will help you get him into a good institution. That'll be the best thing for him."

"Wait a minute," I began. "Mongolism occurs infrequently among Negroes."

"Believe me! I don't know why the resident didn't pick it up in the delivery room—but he's mongoloid alright." His sigh indicated that he'd been through this many times and that he was terribly busy. "You'll have to get used to the idea. Put the child in an institution and avoid the anguish of trying a dozen different doctors. The signs are there. You can't dismiss the signs."

"Doctor, I'd like to talk to you about this."

"What is there to discuss?"

Whether I liked his style or not, I had to admit he was right. There was nothing he could do. Why prolong the conversation?

"Thanks," I said. I heard his end of the line click. "Thanks a whole helluva lot."

Chester Wayne Oden, age two-and-a-half days. Complaint: born with Down's syndrome for reasons unknown. The worst likely sentence: life imprisonment in an "institution." Special conditions: may never talk or walk. May be unable to communicate with any other human being. May be unable to care for himself.

I'd seen the wards where the retarded are kept. Attendants sitting around in their whites, reading the newspapers until something happens. One of the kids messes his pants. Instantly an attendant is there; he cleans up the mess, muttering. The child reaches for his sleeve but is ignored. Other children attempt to play together but fail because one can't see the other, or one can't move himself. Tours of young nurses come through as part of their introduction to the profession, and they stand there, with their faces pressed to the glass. One or two feel ill as their minds begin to register what they've seen. The smart ones have reported in sick today in order to miss this part of their "orientation." The children sit about the room, their heads falling in pools of their own spittle. Some kids try to crawl to a different part of the room for a change of scenery. The hours settle in on the closed room like a motionless day on the desert. Noon is off in the distance, shimmering in the glare, just another point in time when finely chopped food, its flavor long since boiled out, is fed to the children. Mealtime. Hands, jerked momentarily by distractions, drop food onto the hospital smocks, staining them orange for carrots, red for beets, but mostly gray for the potatoes and rice that institution budgets permit.

I tried to picture Wayne on the ward, but the picture wouldn't come to mind. I tried to picture Wayne as a twenty-one year old, propped up to the table. Would he recognize me? Would he understand when I said, "Happy birthday"? Would I have to stuff the cake in his mouth, while he gazed absently in another direction?

Really, Dr. Hampster, what could you expect *anyone* to learn in those wards, much less retarded children?

I began to recall my own days in elementary school. I'd been called "retarded." I'd been sent to a

special school, I guess because I was difficult to handle.
When I went to class for the first time I was scared, and I
knew the way to stay whole was to keep my mouth shut.
I didn't answer the teachers' questions and they began to
get on me. I suppose it was for my own good, but I didn't
know that then. I was sent to a counselor and didn't
say anything there, either. I was told I was dumb,
stupid—retarded. And I believed them. I was too scared
to learn with the class. Everyone seemed to know the
things that the teacher wanted, and I was having a hard
time keeping my head and feelings all tied together.
Finally one teacher, a great giant of a man, approached
me.

"Chester," he said softly as he bent down to face
me, "I expect you to learn what everyone else does. You
can do the work, and I insist you do it. You'll do your
homework tonight!"

"But I can't!" I cried.

His face flushed and he stood up to his full height.
"There is no such word as 'can't' in my class!" he roared.
"You and I will meet tomorrow after hours. Your work
will be done, and we *will* review how well you have
completed it. Understand?"

I nodded to the man and hustled back to my
quarters to do my work. I studied very hard that night.

The next day he looked my work over carefully,
running a huge index finger across each of my penciled
inscriptions. Then he looked at me. "This is satisfactory,
Chester. But I expect the quality to improve. Do you
understand?"

"Yessir," I said. I was relieved not to be
reprimanded and happy to find someone who understood
me. For months we worked together. And finally it
happened; I knew it would.

"Tomorrow," he said one day, "you will report
back to the regular classroom. You are no longer
considered retarded."

I shook his hand. "Thanks," I said, with mixed
feelings. I discovered I was reluctant to leave him.

He had tears in his eyes. "Just remember, Chet.
Never, never let any person tell you that you 'can't.' Can't
just takes a little longer."

As I reflected on those days, I realized how
important it is for any child to live in an atmosphere that

fosters growth, to live with people who care. And I knew that many institutions don't foster anything but vegetation.

There was really no decision to make.

No, sir. We weren't going to institutionalize Wayne. Maybe we might have if I hadn't seen the wards. Or maybe we might have if I hadn't had so much trouble in my own childhood, trying to get on the right track. But I *had* seen the wards, and I *did* remember my own difficulties, and Wayne wasn't going anywhere but home.

I started for Polly's room with determination, but as I approached the door, my feet dragged, and my mind filled with other things to do. I really didn't want to lay this on her. I was afraid she'd think it was her fault. We both knew our son had enough trouble, being black. But this. Talk about being handicapped. This made being black seem easy. I hesitated a bit longer. Then I imagined a nurse coming and popping the news on her. That wouldn't be fair. I had to tell her myself, and I might as well get started.

When I entered the room, Polly was chattering to Wayne, who was busy tanking up on breast, grunting and making a real effort of it. His little short legs pumped away as if he were in a race. Polly looked up and smiled. She was so pleased with herself. "He's so . . ."

I put my finger on her lips. "Don't say it." I watched them for a long time and tried to piece together what I would say. When I looked closely at Wayne I didn't see any gross signs of Down's syndrome. But I also knew Dr. Hampster didn't miss. With surgical precision he had made his objective observations of Wayne and had come to the only possible conclusion. His prescription of a life sentence for Wayne was making it very hard for me to find the right words. I struggled for an hour to tell Polly. Finally, Dr. Anderson walked in and looked the situation over. Like an uncle, he chucked Wayne under the chin. "Have you talked to Dr. Hampster?" he asked me.

"Yeah."

He weighed my tone of voice. "Have you told Polly?"

Polly looked up at me, then to Dr. Anderson. "Told me what?"

Dr. Anderson eyed me questioningly.

"It's not easy," I said.

"Wayne has been identified as a Down's syndrome child," Dr. Anderson explained. Polly frowned her lack of understanding. "Mongolism," Dr. Anderson said gently, and I wondered why I hadn't been able to say that word.

"Now, there are some things you should know about mongolism," Dr. Anderson said to both of us. "First of all, it's not your fault. Neither of you. Remember that. It just happens and we don't know why."

Polly looked down at Wayne. He'd finished his meal and was staring out at the world through his chocolate brown eyes. They say new babies don't see much at first, but Wayne's expression certainly wasn't blank.

Just then Dr. Hampster entered the room. Dr. Anderson thanked him for dropping by and introduced him to Polly.

"I see mother and child are doing well," Hampster said perfunctorily. He picked Wayne up, looking him over clinically. "I want you to know how sorry I am. There are some good institutions . . ."

I must have looked at Hampster the way I'd looked at the locker. Dr. Anderson jumped to my side. "I know how you must feel," Anderson began. "But this doesn't mean you won't have normal children."

Anderson was trying to smooth it over, but Hampster meant for us to hear his message. He spoke with authority, and he looked me straight in the eyes as he talked. "The best thing for your son, the best thing for you and your medical career . . ." He waited for the implication to soak in, "is institutionalization."

I was about to snatch Wayne away from Hampster, but just as I reached for him, Wayne gave me the first of many lessons which would show an intuitive capacity shared by few so-called normal people, including myself. Wayne grimaced, his face turning purple with effort. Thick, greenish-tan exudate ran over the diaper fold and streamed onward, in free fall over Dr. Hampster's white trouser legs and shoes as Wayne completed his bowel movement.

"Right on!" I said to myself. I had been trying to express the writhing in my guts, and Wayne captured it all.

"Our son won't be put in an institution," I said as I took Wayne in my arms. "He's entitled to whatever any new child in my family gets." Polly's look demonstrated her agreement.

Dr. Hampster grimaced. "Your sentiments are commendable, but you must remember that you have others depending on you, too," he lectured. "Furthermore," he added, looking up over his glasses, "your professional career will need a great deal of attention."

"I'll tell you what," I said in measured tones, "Wayne will stay in our home until it becomes injurious to his health. Or until his presence, for whatever reason, jeopardizes someone else."

Dr. Anderson stepped forward. "This has come all of a sudden," he said. "I'm sure we all want to think carefully about this decision."

"The decision isn't that tough," I said with finality.

Dr. Hampster frowned at me. "I know how you must feel," he said, turning to go. "We all like to think we sire perfect specimens. But accidents of nature happen."

I wondered how many people would regard my son that way—as an accident of nature who would obstruct our life, as a limit to our convenience. I wondered if parents of other Down's syndrome children felt that way. I held Wayne a little tighter. A nurse tapped me on the shoulder and motioned that she'd change Wayne's diapers.

"No thanks," I said, "I'd rather." Carefully, I washed Wayne's anus and genitals while he screamed at the top of his lungs. "Hey, man," I said to him, "I'm beginning to like you. You really have a way of getting right to the issue."

CHAPTER TWO

A couple of months after Wayne was born, Barney Newton's old Studebaker pulled up in front of our house, and Barney leaned over the back seat to rummage for a large gallon jar.

Barney viewed the world with the aplomb of a mechanic who tunes a Corvette with a pipe wrench and a crow bar. He was in his internship and already applying for residency in gynecology. Like myself, Barney was an ex-G.I., older than most interns, and turned on by chemistry. Barney pulled good marks, but his talents were practical rather than theoretical. His chemistry skills, for example, were focused on producing a cheap but palatable alcohol in the organic chemistry class he taught, without being discovered by his students or his supervisor. At this moment, Barney was bringing over his latest batch for testing.

By the time he got in the door, I had ice, orange juice, and glasses set out for him. He danced around the kitchen mixing drinks before he flopped at the table and kicked up his feet. "Oden," he began suddenly, "what have I come here to tell you?"

I pulled pensively at my chin. "You've discovered a cure for jock itch called 'Scratch It.'"

"You're great," he moaned. "You're beautiful. I come over here, my heart laden with sorrow, and you're being jocular."

"That's terrible," I chuckled at his pun.

"I've just been rejected by Eberwood Hospital and Torrance General. How am I going to get into gynecology if they won't even give me a *chance?*"

"Hell! I wouldn't let you near my carburetor!"

"Okay, okay, sensitive physician." Barney shrugged and mixed himself another. "I'll send for some more applications and fill them out in English."

"You're giving in," I laughed. "You can always change your language. That's easier than changing the color of your skin."

"Keep up the grades," Barney said. "You'll get in. Minority students are becoming collectors' items."

Barney had brought along some Cracker Jacks for the three kids. When Polly came in to greet him, carrying Wayne, his eyes settled on the new addition. "Hey," he said, "I forgot to bring something for the new Oden. Boy or girl?"

Funny how it is, when you're a working student. You don't have a pot to piss in, but it doesn't make any difference. No one you know is any better off. You just assume friends are going to stay for dinner. And they do. So, without taking a break in the conversation, Polly put together a pot of "stew," student terminology for leftovers watered down and re-boiled for the third time. All the while, she was suckling Wayne and talking to Barney.

Although I'd always admired Barney, I hadn't really understood him. He was not only terribly talented, he had power behind him which he refused to recognize. Barney had been offered a law degree on a silver platter, but he was too busy under the hood of his old Studebaker to bother picking it up. He wrote a paper in philosophy that earned him recognition and offers from several major universities, but he laughed and said the paper wasn't even serious. Encouraged to step into the family firm, Barney preferred the stench of test tubes. And just in the last year, Barney had begun to show real interest in residency. His only problem had been in deciding which specialty to select.

As I watched him now, I could begin to understand ol' Barney a bit. We were pretty well through our third screwdrivers, and I was less tense than usual, moving toward relaxed. I began to observe Barney eyeing Wayne with an intensity that went far beyond casual interest in someone else's child. A frown pulled at Barney's eyebrows, and he moved just perceptibly forward. He chatted with Polly in a very casual way, but his observations weren't quick or superficial. He played "patty cake" with Wayne's hands and examined them. He tickled Wayne, played "bee landing on the nose," and clucked in Wayne's ear. When Barney was done, he reconstructed a couple of drinks. "Healthy dude," he remarked noncommittally.

I held up my glass in silent thanks to him and looked steadily into Barney's pale gray windows. "Thanks for the house call," I said.

"Whatdya mean?"

"Have you thought of pediatrics?" I asked him.

"Sure—I *thought* about it. But children don't pay their bills."

Then Barney looked from Wayne to me and raised his eyebrows questioningly. I nodded ever so slightly that yes, of course I knew what he was talking about, and he relaxed back in his chair.

"What differences have you noticed between Wayne and the other three?" Barney said easily to Polly.

Polly stirred the stew without missing a beat. She didn't even look at Barney as she spoke, though once she tossed him a sidelong glance to see if he was sober. "Oh, there's not really much difference," she said, fondling Wayne lovingly. "He has a stronger grasp reflex than the others, and he babbles more than either Earl or Terry did." She took the stew from the stove and began to ladle it into bowls. "C'mon, children," she called in a voice that brought an immediate scampering of feet and the children's appearance. "The doctors have said some things about him, but you know how doctors are. They'll tell you something one time and deny it the next."

My God, I thought, Polly, where is your head? Barney had gotten up to spike a couple of glasses of orange juice, and Polly declined because she didn't want to sour her milk. I'd known Polly for two years now and had never seen her duck an issue. The only thing she couldn't tolerate was not hearing the truth. But here she was, as blasé as a cat in the creamery, telling us that the doctors were flat out wrong, that there was nothing wrong with Wayne, even though Hampster had identified eight signs of Down's syndrome in front of her. At the time of the diagnosis, we had all nodded our agreement, not because it was pleasant, but because it seemed to square with the facts. But not Polly!

I guess I'd been into my own head so deeply these
past few days that it hadn't occurred to me that Polly
might have strong feelings about Wayne which disagreed
with mine. She already had three normal children—no,
they were *super*-normal. I wondered if she harbored any
secret feelings against me or blamed me for Wayne's
condition.

I wondered myself if I had some hidden fault. But
I'd read about Down's syndrome, and all the information
I found indicated that Wayne was simply an unfortunate
victim, a person whose protoplasm had begun in a
strange, accidental way, and whose life would be the
unfolding of this accident.

Polly didn't need to prove to the world that she
could produce a bright, healthy child. So why should
she reject the medical opinion that Wayne had Down's
syndrome?

"You don't believe the docs," I said pensively. I
wasn't trying to bug her. I was trying to understand.

Polly sat down to the table and faced me directly.
Her tone was straightforward. "Believe the docs what?"
she said.

"C'mon, you know what they said about Wayne."

Her gaze was steady. "I heard about the Down's
syndrome." She ate a bit of stew. "It's a little thin," she
acknowledged, then went on, "but what does that
mean?"

"Well," I began, "it has a lot of implications."

Polly stopped me. "Wayne does everything the
other three did. He's a little bigger and stronger. I don't
know what else it means."

I looked from Barney to Polly. He was following us
like a man watching a tennis match. "Wayne will
develop . . . a little differently from the other three," I
said.

"We'll see," she said, digging into her stew. "We'll
see."

When Wayne finished his meal he was restless, so
Polly swung him over to me.

I began rocking Wayne, and his face broke into a
happy grin. Absently, I slowed the motion of my arms to
a stop and Wayne's smile faded as if in response, like a
drop of water on hot pavement. When I resumed
swinging he gave out a deep, throaty giggle, but the

17

laughter died when I stopped again, and Wayne scowled
in disappointment.

"Hey, look!" I said to the others. They watched as I
rocked Wayne, who giggled on cue. I stopped, and
Wayne looked as though he'd bitten into a lemon.

"My turn," Barney laughed. He stroked Wayne's
foot, bottom and side, and gently poked a finger into his
middle. Wayne's reflexes didn't seem well established,
and Barney looked at me. "Fat little devil," he said, as his
finger disappeared into Wayne's stomach.

"Hypotonic muscles," I added, "and diffused
breathing."

Barney found one of the kids' Cracker Jacks and
held it out to Wayne. Wayne looked at it curiously but
showed no active interest in eating it. Then Barney
stroked his cheek, and Wayne's mouth popped open.
Barney rubbed the Cracker Jack across Wayne's tongue.
That was like pressing the "go" button. Wayne lit up,
giggled, and started squirming. When Barney took it
away, the lights went out. He gave it to Wayne again, and
Wayne sucked on it, squirmed, and giggled.

"Hey, you aren't so dumb after all," Barney
laughed. He turned the Cracker Jack around so Wayne
could get all the caramel.

Now that's Barney. He tells it like he sees it. You
don't get mad at Barney; if you don't like to hear it as he
sees it, you don't have him over for supper.

Polly looked at Barney and me and shook her head
in mild exasperation. "Maybe there's hope," she said.
"Maybe. But you both sound worse than those medical
professors in the University Hospital that don't see
children except under a magnifying glass. Sure Wayne is
fat. He eats more than the other three ever did. Of course
he can respond, and of course he likes to be rocked and
fondled, and he likes sweet things. You two act like
you've never seen a child before! Where have you been?"

I looked at Barney, and he looked at me. "You
know, Polly, you're right," Barney said. "Everyone gets
all hung up on their little piece of the world. It's very easy
to get into your own thing and forget there are a lot of
plain, old, ordinary people who need help once in a
while. I agree—I mean it. It's times like this I think of
going into general practice."

I looked at him dubiously. "Sure," I said, "the only

reason you'd do that is because it's the only specialty you can spell." We all laughed.

Then Barney said to Wayne, "See ya, little buddy. Hang in there, and when I get done, I'll do your tonsils and adenoids, patch your knees, and bandage the elbows."

A few weeks later, something happened that made me believe Polly was more concerned about Wayne than she let on to Barney and me. Or at least more interested in the medical aspects of his development. I came home from school a little early one day and found a quiet house. My house—quiet! That event was noteworthy in itself, and I'm not sure if it will ever happen again. It was a pretty summer afternoon and the bigger kids were out playing. Polly apparently had no visitors. When I went inside, the place almost echoed my footsteps. I stopped short and peered around, hesitant to break the unexpected silence. The bedroom door was closed. I walked very quietly over, twisted the knob carefully, and opened it without a sound. There was Polly on the edge of the bed, with Wayne lying on his back and cooing to her as she stroked him with one hand. Her other hand traced the lines of a thick pediatrics text. She looked at the book and then at Wayne's palms, measuring the length of his fingers, one by one, and comparing the lines across the inside of his hand to her own. Then she looked at his feet and toes and back at the book. She frowned deliberately, then looked at Wayne's forehead, opened his mouth and peered inside. She examined his face and eyes and mouth thoroughly. If she was checking out the signs for Down's syndrome noted in the medical manual, she was doing a thorough job. But I didn't know for sure, and I didn't ask her.

"Hi," I said in a cheery voice, as if I had just burst into the house. "I got off a little early." Polly slammed the book shut and set it back on the shelf.

"How's school?" she asked.

If Polly chose not to talk about Wayne's condition, I would honor that, but I wondered how concerned she really was.

I ran into Dr. Anderson a few days later and laid it out to him. Down's syndrome was not Dr. Anderson's specialty, but he had heard a good bit about the problems of parents with Down's syndrome children. He put a hand on my shoulder. "You know what I'd prescribe if I were your family doctor?"

"You're the closest thing to it," I said.

"Have another baby! Right away."

I stuck my finger in my ear and pretended to clear an obstruction from it.

"No!" he laughed. "You heard me right. Have another baby. Parents of Down's syndrome children often think there is something wrong with themselves. They can have some pretty unfortunate reactions to things that are in no way their fault."

I looked at him closely for a moment. "Okay," I said finally, "you nailed that one! Maybe it would be good for both of us!"

He slapped me encouragingly on the back. I started to go, but he held me. "One more thing." He scribbled a number on a piece of paper. "Call this number. Belongs to a friend of mine. She has a Down's syndrome son and lives near you. A visit might help Polly, too."

I thought about it for a moment. Sometimes you begin to think you are the only one in the world with problems. "Hey, sounds like a good idea!" I said. "You know, you're wasting your talent here in these sterile halls."

"They aren't that sterile," Anderson said, and he was gone.

Joyce Severensen had a soft, sweet voice over the telephone, and her looks matched her voice. She seemed delighted to come over and visit with her son, Donny. Polly had made a big lunch, even though she was reluctant about the whole meeting. But Joyce took away any tension that might have built up. She came in, handed her coat to me, and told Donny to take off his shoes. Then she turned around and flashed her soft, slightly sad brown eyes at me. "You know," she laughed gently, "Donny is a cheerful boy, but sometimes when he's frustrated he kicks, and his hard shoes can hurt. So I take away his weapons when he visits."

I thought about giving Donny's weapons back to him. I wouldn't want anyone disarming *me* if I went visiting. But Donny didn't seem upset, and I knew Joyce had more important things to do than argue over protocol.

"May I see your child?" she asked easily. Polly went to our bedroom for Wayne. "Isn't he big!" Joyce exclaimed.

Polly managed a hint of a smile. "Yes. We had quite a time with him!"

"You know," Joyce said matter of factly, "there *are* some similarities to Donny." She continued to look down at Wayne. Then she took him in her arms, poked and prodded him. "But there are many differences, too. Your child is rounder; he doesn't have the pigeon breast or square hands like Donny."

Polly stood on one foot and then the other, trying to reach for Wayne politely, and Joyce, reading her gestures, handed him back.

Joyce was very easy about the children. She brought Donny over to her chair, and Polly began to unwind a little. "Look at Donny," Joyce said, hugging him. "He has the distinctive eyes—almost Asian, and he's square and solid in his shoulders, short and stocky." She tickled Donny as she talked, and he giggled with pleasure. "He likes to run and play, and we've found that special hard soles make it easier for him. As you can see, he's a bit toed-in and awkward."

Polly just stared at Joyce. She nodded in response to Joyce's comments, but her eyes opened in amazement at Joyce's relaxed attitude toward Donny.

"He's our third child," Joyce continued, "and we have a younger girl. But Donny's our baby. He's still our love bug."

Polly's eyes darted from Joyce to me. I could guess at the questions which leapt to her mind, but she didn't ask them. A light silence fell as we watched Donny. We had long since baby-proofed our house, and Joyce seemed to know that, letting him bounce around the living room, bang into chairs, and feign being hurt. Then, in triumph, he'd bounce up and go off roaring again. After a while, he disappeared into the back rooms. I raised a hand to indicate to Joyce that she shouldn't be alarmed, and soon, out came Mila and Terry, ushering Donny in front of them. They had dressed Donny up in a long skirt and big, floppy hat. Donny laughed the whole time, and Mila and Terry ordered him about as if they were the wicked stepsisters and he were Cinderella. The more he'd do, the more they'd ask him to do. I glanced at Joyce.

"He'll let them know when he's had enough," she said.

As Joyce prepared to leave, I realized that she had succeeded in showing us that parenting a Down's child could be as natural as parenting any other child. Her easy attitude had calmed us.

Just as she was leaving, she became serious. "You know," she said, "I guess we all put a little more into working with Donny. I don't know why—it just seems to happen. Maybe it's because of him or maybe it's because of us . . . or maybe it's because he might not be with us as long as the other children."

"Did you ever think of putting him in an institution?"

"If you didn't think about that once, you'd probably be kidding yourself," Joyce conceded. "Yes, we had advice . . . pressure to do that. From our doctor and from family. In fact, we had decided to. But when we had to start making arrangements, neither George nor I could pick up the telephone. I can't say for anyone else, but for us there really wasn't a choice."

"Hey, thanks for coming," I said.

She nodded. "If you hear of another couple who has a Down's baby, go visit them."

"Sure," I said. "Count on it."

I don't know whether the visit from Joyce changed us, or whether the Odens just started getting smart. But we began to recover from the shock of Wayne's birth.

Polly went on a kick, learning Wayne's vocalizations. I bought her a tape recorder and she began recording him under various circumstances. Like, in the mornings Wayne was very vocal; he seemed to want to sing for his breakfast. Polly often put off his feeding five minutes just to get more recordings. I challenged her about what she was doing with them. "Learning about Wayne," she said simply. She played a recording of him cooing and chirping in the morning. "He talks much more than Earl or Mila did."

"You think he's more vocal," I said.

She put her ear close to the speaker so she could hear all the nuances of the tape. "He talks lots more," she said without looking at me, "but he uses mostly 'a' sounds, and he doesn't have any of the 'e's.'" Then she giggled to herself. "Listen carefully to these two recordings and tell me when he did them," she said. As she played the tape, I heard Wayne saying "gaa gaa gaa" with considerable earnestness. The next recording was the same intent gaa gaa gaaing.

"But can't you tell the difference?" she asked.

She played them again, and I listened intently for the second time. The third time around, the light came on. On one recording he ga gaad several tones higher than on the other. "He's listening to the radio?" I guessed.

"Listen," Polly said, leaning closer to the tape recorder. "Listen carefully." She played a recording of her own voice that was followed by a higher-pitched gu-guing. Then she played a portion where I'd spoken, and this was followed by a lower-pitched gu-guing.

"I'll be damned," I said. "The little character is mimicking us."

Polly became pregnant shortly after Wayne's first birthday, while I was still attending medical school. The two events weren't really related, except that now I had a greater incentive to finish so I could support and enjoy the brood that began to issue forth from our union.

My first tour of duty was in the emergency room at L.A. General Hospital with an experimental emergency rescue unit. I was excited when I first heard about it, but after a week, I discovered that the word "externship" was just another term for slave labor. We were usually assigned a ninety-hour week in addition to filling in when any of the regular staff or interns were unable to report.

I really didn't have a lot of time to spend observing Wayne. Oh, I tried. But as often as not the beeper in my pocket would sound off, and even before I got to the telephone, I was hollering to Polly that I was on my way to the hospital and didn't know what time I'd be home. So while Polly was there all the time and saw Wayne from moment to moment, I saw him more like from week to week.

About that time, Wayne started walking on his little roly-poly legs. His barrel belly rocked as he swayed from side to side. Polly was excited with his progress. We had been told that he wouldn't walk until much later, probably well past his second birthday. So again, hope was kindled in Polly that Wayne might be "normal."

Spurred by Wayne's unexpected interest in perambulation, Polly walked him as much as he would and encouraged him to extend his command of pedal activity. She worked on his walking sideways and backwards and his standing on one foot. Polly, as close as she was to Wayne, saw progress in his motor development that I really couldn't detect. I just couldn't see all the "progress" that she talked about. But I didn't want to discourage her. Ha! That was fortunate, because I couldn't have succeeded if I'd wanted to. So I patiently waited and watched for the hints of progress Polly so confidently forecast. Occasionally, I thought I saw him display one of his new "skills," such as the backward step Polly had "taught" him, but it would be a tentative move, and I was often unsure of my observation. Certainly Wayne advanced in motor development, but I didn't know whether Polly looked at that objectively or simply interpreted it to conform to her own longing.

As Polly grew rounder with our second child, she spent long hours reading about motor and speech development in children. And she began talking more and more to Wayne. "He can't say what he hasn't heard," she said to me, like a professor of linguistics. "You have to provide the model so he can mimic it." From my once-in-awhile observations of Wayne, I'd swear that he really did begin "talking" a lot more, even if that meant he was uttering vocalizations I couldn't understand.

"You just aren't around enough," Polly laughed at me. She seemed to know everything Wayne was saying. Polly and Wayne would babble and coo at each other for long periods, and suddenly Polly would get up and get him something to eat or change him. That was communication I guess, but I had no idea how she understood his "urps" and "gubs" and "daahs."

I was sitting at home on one of the few evenings when I ate an entire dinner without being called out, just enjoying dessert and reading the paper, when I heard Polly say something.

"Huh?" I said.

"Oh, I didn't mean to disturb you," she said, "I was talking to Wayne."

I looked around. No Wayne.

"Are you playing games?" she said.

I put the paper down. "Why would I play games?"

Polly laughed lightly. "Not you. Wayne."

Again I looked around. I got up and looked behind chairs and under the table. "When was the last time you had your eyes checked?" I asked her.

"Oh, I get it," she said. She went out of the room and was soon back with Wayne toddling behind her. "What game are you playing?" she asked.

"Ah, daah ah gunk!"

Polly was folding clothes fresh from the drier. "Now say 'Uh duh bunk.'"

"Ah, daah dah oog."

"Oh, very good," Polly enjoined him.

I looked over. That was good? Okay, I said to myself, stay out of the way of progress. I went back to the second page.

* * *

Eric was born smaller than Wayne, and compared to this new arrival, two-year-old Wayne was incredibly talented. He was much more mobile than Eric and better at communicating, even with his "ahs" and "oogs." For the first few months, Eric cried rather well for a small child, but there were really no sounds to compare with those of the very verbal Wayne.

I continued to be overwhelmed by the externship even as I moved from the L.A. General emergency room to the Torrance one. But when I was around, I often saw Polly taping Wayne's verbalizations. "Here," she'd say, "is the beginning of a plosive." I could hear Wayne babbling, and if I was relaxed, I could almost stretch his sounds to fit Polly's description. If I wanted a comparison I went to Eric's room and listened to his noises: crying, snorts, heavy breathing, grunts, and squeals. Yes, I agreed with Polly. Wayne was really tremendously advanced over Eric.

Meanwhile, Earl, Mila, and Terry had taken over Wayne. When Polly wasn't giving him developmental exercises or recording his vocalizations, the older children spent a lot of time with him for his entertainment, but as far as I could see, for theirs also. This left Eric to himself, and Polly and I really couldn't let Eric grow up an orphan. So she became pregnant again.

Eric was a little over a year old when Polly delivered the twins, and he still wasn't walking or babbling as much as Wayne. I think the excitement of the twins' birth deflected Polly's attention from Wayne's development for a few weeks, perhaps two months, and during those weeks Eric began to catch up with Wayne, to walk and to speak his first words. Eric's articulation seemed to improve by quantum leaps every time I saw him, while Wayne had reached a plateau. I didn't really have time to discuss this with Polly during the twins' delivery or the adjustment period following. I wasn't sure she'd agree with me anyway. My observations were based on limited time with Wayne, and I knew that excitement has an odd, temporary effect on children's development. I really didn't want to make a big deal out of it, so I waited for a better opportunity.

Barney Newton had heard of the Oden additions and brought over a shopping bag half full of Cracker Jacks and half full of his latest achievement in the production of Newton's brew. Barney had switched fields again and was now through a year of psychiatric residency.

When he came into the kitchen, all the Odens assembled there; that is, those who could walk or toddle. Wayne was the only one who ventured forward, almost crushing Barney's leg in a big hug. Barney picked Wayne up and tickled him. "Wow! Look at this big guy! How's ol' Wayne doing?"

Wayne loved it. He giggled and talked a mile a minute to Barney, none of it intelligible as far as I could tell. Eric, shying away from Barney, clung to Polly.

"Mine," Eric said, spying the Cracker Jacks. There it was for me. Typical of the two boys—Wayne, a mile a minute, and Eric, one precise word.

Polly must have read my mind. "Don't you think Wayne's developing rapidly?" she asked Barney.

"Fine, just fine," Barney said. He picked up Eric, who was momentarily terrified. "And another fine young Oden." Barney looked him over with a quick, professional eye. "Very handsome youngster," he said.

Barney then went in the other room to see the twins. When he came back out, his eyes were drawn to Wayne. "Y'know," he said, "I spend a lot of my time in institutions. Terrible places. Don't do much for people, really. I think many doctors could get distorted views of child development if they only saw institutionalized children—normal or retarded."

I mixed Barney and myself a screwdriver. "Maybe that's one of the problems in doctoring at a university hospital," I suggested. "Too easy to get experience only with kids who've been cooped up in hospital conditions. The docs don't see what development is like in a natural environment."

Barney nodded. "Kids die in sterile environments. They need that old mother love, even from a lousy mother."

Polly was following our dialogue carefully.

"I want you to hear some tapes," she said. "I want your professional opinion on whether Wayne's speech is becoming clearer." She got our recorder and played some portions as she described the sounds.

"Hey," Barney said, "he certainly is coming along."

"And look at his walking," Polly said. "Isn't he advanced—or well along—compared with . . . just any child?"

"He certainly is big and strong," Barney said. "You've really done a good job with him."

Polly didn't catch Barney's compliment to her. But I really had to agree with him. Polly had Wayne coming along nicely. Sometimes in my weaker moments I almost shared her secret wish and hope. And sometimes I talked about it with other people.

Doc Anderson had listened to me several times when I was down, on those occasions when I'd talked about Wayne's progress to him. Though he admitted he was no expert on Down's, he was interested in Wayne, nonetheless. He asked Polly to bring Wayne to the hospital for a sort of "get reacquainted" visit.

The fact that Doc Anderson delivered Wayne, Eric, and recently Michael and Markel, may have had something to do with his interest. But I believe there was more to it than that. In spite of his training in the impersonal atmosphere of the University Hospital, Doc Anderson was a humanistic man. And although he might not admit it, I'm sure he winced every time Hampster said, "Hospitalize that child." Dr. Anderson wasn't a crusader like me. But I believed he would look at Wayne as an individual rather than as a medical stereotype.

When we arrived with Wayne at Anderson's outer office, Polly was armed with her tape recorder and recordings. She was ready to go, but he asked us to wait for a moment. Then he whispered to the nurse, who got on the horn. In moments, I heard the page: "Dr. Hampster, call the operator. Dr. Hampster, call the operator."

Doc Anderson exchanged greetings with Polly and Wayne. "How are the twins?" he asked as he put his arm around Polly and walked her into his office, chatting about babies and leaving me to carry the paraphernalia. Just as we became comfortable, Dr. Hampster walked in, thin as a razor. The slash of his mouth barely moved as he spoke. "The Oden child!" he said, with profundity.

"One of the seven!" Anderson answered, half smiling.

"Are any of the others Down's syndrome?" Hampster began, with the formal tone of a prosecuting attorney.

"No," Doc Anderson said firmly, assuming control of the meeting. "Mrs. Oden has some information to share with us."

Polly got out her twenty-dollar electronic equipment and slipped the cassette into place. From it came a string of Wayne's vocalizations. Polly referred to her notes. "Here," she said, clearing her throat, "is Wayne talking at eighteen months; first to his daddy . . ." She stopped and looked nervously at Hampster. "To Dr. Oden," she corrected. "Now," she said, gaining courage, "to me." She played the excerpts once and then instructed them to note the pitch differences as she played the recordings again. Next came Wayne's verbal play before breakfast. Finally, Polly played a tape of Wayne repeating the sounds he heard from her at twenty-four months and again six months later.

Anderson pursed his lips. He turned to Hampster. "What do you think?" he asked cautiously.

Hampster's expression was unchanged. "The fidelity of the recording equipment isn't what it could be," he said in an unexpected show of generosity. "But I heard the primitive vocalizations."

Anderson cleared his throat. "Didn't you hear the improvement in inflection and pronunciation?"

Hampster smiled condescendingly at Anderson. "Did you? Really? I heard immature speech patterns. Perhaps you heard something else. I suggest that wishful thinking is distorting what we hear."

"Hey," I said slowing things down, "play it again. Now *listen*."

Hampster looked at the ceiling during the replay.

I turned to Dr. Anderson. "No great articulation. But far beyond what we expected for . . ." I paused, manipulating the machine, "his age and diagnosis."

Anderson nodded. "I'm impressed." He turned to me then and shook his head. "But I'm too close to Wayne. I'm almost part of the family and certainly no impartial observer!"

But Polly and I weren't finished yet. I took Wayne and set him in the middle of the group. "Go to Dr. Anderson," I said. I realized that if Wayne walked to Dr. Anderson, it would mean he had heard and understood my request. We all watched as Wayne turned from me to Polly. Uncertainly, he toddled as if off-balance; he turned to me, then staggered over to Dr. Anderson. Polly and I exchanged glances.

"I don't know what you're trying to prove," Hampster shrugged. "He followed your cues, if you want a *reasonable* explanation. But is that what you want? Haven't you come here to to prove to me, and therefore to yourselves, that Wayne isn't a Down's child? I can understand your desire to do that, but I question your judgment. Just what are your actions doing to Wayne? He may have unusual skills for a Down's syndrome child—in hearing, understanding, and carrying out directions—or he may simply have gone to the person who was nearest him, with a few prods by you."

I sighed. He was partly right. But there was another reason we were here. "You would concede, however, wouldn't you, Dr. Hampster, that he is showing remarkable development at home and that for him home is better than an institution?"

Hampster looked surprised. "Indeed!" He took off his glasses and cleaned them. "You're letting your emotions get in the way of your rational decisions, Dr. Oden! Very dangerous for a man who avows interest in the medical profession. Certainly the best place for Wayne is in an institution where he can get the proper care and treatment. And," he replaced his glasses, "where he'll not drain your energies, which should more appropriately be channeled into professional activities."

"To hospitalize Wayne for the convenience of the medical profession?" Polly was angered for just an instant, and I could see the daughter of the physician in that flash. "That, sir, is misuse of the profession!" Just as quickly, she submerged her feelings.

Anderson smiled uneasily. "Don't you think, Dr. Hampster, that under certain circumstances a Down's child should remain at home?"

Dr. Hampster was still cool. "Most certainly!" he said, "when the parents cannot afford the bill, or when they have nothing better to do but tend a child of severe limitations!"

That did it. I saw red. "Doctor . . . ah, Doctor . . ." For the moment I forgot his name. "I've heard that you . . . shall we say . . . encouraged your mother into a home for the aged. Is Wayne just another opportunity for you to justify your own actions?"

The room fell silent. Hampster glared at me, and I felt my knees turn to water. "The name is Dr. Hampster," he said evenly. "I'm sure you'll recall the name time and again as you apply for residency. Good day, Dr. Anderson." He slammed the door behind him.

There wasn't a whole lot to say. I gathered up Wayne and Polly and our equipment. "Thanks, Dr. Anderson," I said. He nodded, and closed the door softly behind us.

It was a long ride home. I could hear Wayne gurgling in the back seat. I drove slowly so I wouldn't hit anybody in my anger.

When we got home, we turned Wayne loose and collapsed in the kitchen chairs. I popped my knuckles as I thought about Dr. Hampster. Polly put her hands over mine in a silent gesture that told me not to worry. But I *had* to worry.

Meanwhile, Wayne toddled through the house to see who was home. He found the other kids, squealed delight, and wandered into the kitchen. Then he headed for the refrigerator and stood there patiently. Wayne's patience wore quickly, though, and soon he began to bang on the door of the fridge. Polly and I looked all around the room as if we didn't see or hear him.

"Where's Wayne?" Polly asked. "Have you seen him?" Wayne gave the door another rap and then some real solid blows.

"Ooog, oog," he bubbled.

"Oh, there you are," Polly feigned. "What on earth could you want?"

"Baah, op," Wayne continued, as he banged on the door for good measure.

Polly opened the door. Wayne pointed inside with his short, stubby finger and grunted deep in his throat.

"Oh, you want an apple," she said, pretending ignorance of his wants. She got an apple and extended it to him.

Wayne stomped his foot. "Pay!" he burst out, and pointed into the fridge.

"Milk!" Polly said and got the bottle out.

"Pay!" Wayne insisted and pulled at her skirt, pointing up at the shelf of the fridge.

Polly said aloud, "Let's see, what does that little boy want?" After moving several jars about, she took out a dish of peaches and put them on the table. Wayne followed her to the table and tried without success to look up and over the edge. He stood there, mouth open, a healthy stream of saliva spilling out over his lips. He batted his eyes and strained up on the tips of his toes.

Polly smiled down at him. "Would you like some peaches?"

Wayne began a little dance and became so excited at the thought of peaches that he lifted both feet off the floor at once and landed on his fanny. He sat there on the floor, flailing his legs in an effort to regain his feet and continued to reach up for the peaches he knew to be on the obscured table top. Polly pulled the high chair over to the table. As Wayne began to climb into the high chair, I rendered assistance whenever I thought he might miss a step and fall on his head. Finally secured in his seat, Wayne reached into the bowl of peaches and extracted several pieces with each hand. He brought his fist to his mouth, squeezing the peaches as juice squirted between his fingers, ran down his arm, and dripped from his elbow to the floor.

When Wayne finished his peaches, he sat in his chair, quite satisfied, licking his chops and beaming out at the world.

"You know," Polly said, "he'll always need more attention, more love and care, than any of the others."

"It's a relief to hear you say that," I said.

"I never said he wasn't *different*." For a moment, Polly's temper blazed. "God makes each one of us different. It is as it is, and we must accept it and live with it."

We sat together in silence, watching the sun settle into the cool of the evening. Then Polly rose. "Come on, Wayne," she said. "Off to bed with you." I wandered into the living room and flopped into my reading chair.

But I didn't read. I watched as Polly checked in each bedroom to see that the big kids were settled down and that Eric and the twins were sleeping. Finally, she went into our room where Wayne lay gurgling in his crib. She threw an extra blanket on him and spoke to him in a slow, sweet tone. I saw the lights go out in his room.

After Polly joined me in the living room, she picked up some darning and set to work. In about three minutes she was asleep.

CHAPTER THREE

When Wayne was born, I had wondered what we'd done to deserve the tragedy of his handicap. That feeling faded as we began to think of Wayne as a person and not a diagnosis. As Wayne grew, I began to wonder what he had done wrong to deserve *me*. Sometimes I couldn't believe my own incompetence at fathering.

We'd been told that Wayne would have impaired vision because he was a Down's child. But we began to suspect he had additional vision problems when he was about six. As Wayne's eye-hand coordination improved, he was more able to grab those things near his face than those farther away. He would scowl at things when they were several feet away, but not when they were within a foot or so of his face.

Dumb me!

As if Wayne didn't have enough handicaps, we'd remained insensitive to his near-sightedness. Once I realized this, I could imagine Wayne struggling with the visual world, trying to make sense of fuzzy blobs unpredictably appearing and fading through the haze.

Normally, I'd have had a six- or eight-week wait for an eye examination. But when I laid Wayne's case on the eye docs, they squeezed him in the next day. They put Wayne through a lot of fancy tests I hadn't seen before, trying to determine just how near-sighted Wayne really was. By shining a narrow beam of light into his eyes, the ophthalmologists could closely approximate the degree to which Wayne's eyes were out-of-focus and the correction required in a pair of glasses for him. All this without even asking Wayne to look at charts.

I was really happy with the way the docs worked with Wayne. By the end of the examination, everyone there had something nice to say to him. I guess they easily discovered that Wayne would rather laugh than anything else in life, and the entire staff got to know him.

The second time I brought Wayne to the eye clinic, the staff took the measurements for his frames. They just knew Wayne wasn't going to let regular rims and glasses sit on his ears and nose, so they built him some goggles that held the glasses firmly in place. The lenses looked to be two inches thick and made his eyes appear to be the size of BB's. From my side of his glasses, they didn't do much for his appearance. But from the other side, wow! I could only observe and draw my own conclusions.

As soon as the doc fit them on Wayne's head, Wayne looked at me. For a long moment he just stared, blinking. Then he broke into a big, picket-fence smile and reached for my face. I came close so he could touch the stubble of my beard and pull the lids of my eyes and poke his finger up my nose. I wondered if he was seeing me clearly for the first time. He pulled my hair and giggled as he unwound one of the tightly curled tufts. Then he looked at me and laughed.

"Hey, Wayne," I chuckled, "you have to go home with us whether you like our looks or not." When Wayne heard everyone laugh, he broke into another broad grin. Then he tugged at his new glasses. I took them off for a moment, and he pulled for them to be replaced. He blinked and stared, then started to clap his hands and kick his feet all at the same time.

"Thanks," I said to the docs, "for giving him two eyes. If he can see to eat better now, I may come back and have you fog them up a little!"

Wayne ran over to the wall and touched it with his finger tips. He tasted it with his tongue, made a bad face, and looked at it again.

Outside, Wayne saw some birds, jumped up and down, and ran after them. He looked up at the trees, staring at the patterns the leaves made against the sky until I got a crick in my neck just watching him.

For a week, Wayne didn't want to be held, and he didn't have much time for hugging or kissing either. He was too busy looking over his world.

The thing that really impressed Wayne was the neighbor's big dog. The dog was fenced in behind a "Beware" sign, and Wayne hadn't been within thirty feet of the big, mobile, gray and black beast. When Wayne first saw it, he stood rigidly still. When the dog made a move to come over by us, Wayne climbed up my leg. He had probably not anticipated the dimensions of a full-grown German shepherd, so he stood there, rigid, eyes fixed on it. Finally, when he saw the dog was friendly, Wayne began to relax. He extended his hand through the fence. The dog, tail wagging, came sniffing over to investigate.

With his glasses Wayne never again got sweaty over animals. In fact, he developed a real liking for them, *all* kinds of them.

For his birthday, he got a stuffed, furry frog. Don't ask me how he got a stuffed frog. I'm not against frogs, or even tadpoles, and I can understand kids getting off on teddy bears and furry rabbits and lambs. But frogs? Well, Wayne got himself a green, stuffed frog, and he loved it. He soon discovered the pleasure of rubbing the frog's fur against his lips. Many nights he went to sleep, rubbing that damned frog against his lips and humming to himself.

Eric, who was quick to seize opportunities, had developed a game which involved sneaking up on Wayne and grabbing the frog from him. Wayne would naturally get up to reclaim his prized possession, and Eric would take off to other parts of the house. Wayne was much slower than Eric, and the game lasted either as long as Eric wanted it to, or until Wayne finally set up a howl to make someone intervene.

The game pattern was broken by our youngest son, Chris, now a year old. Chris was easily dissatisfied with the ways of the world. He wanted to know where everyone was and what they were doing; if they weren't doing it right, he was upset.

One morning when Chris woke up, he must have sensed that things weren't just so, and he set up a howl. Wayne, who held his frog, as usual, watched Chris pensively for several minutes. Evidently, Chris's crying stirred something in him, for Wayne walked over to Chris and began stroking him with the frog. Chris, for a

moment, was silent. Then he started in again. Wayne
tentatively pushed the frog into Chris's arms, and Chris
stopped crying to examine the furry thing that had been
thrust upon him. Then, following Wayne's example,
Chris began stroking himself with the frog. His tears
gone, Chris seemed finally content.

Wayne, now deprived of his source of comfort,
plunged his thumb in his mouth. He reached out and
picked up a brightly colored piece of paper that hadn't
reached the wastebasket. It was red and green on one
side, and Wayne stared at it, then turned it over and saw
that the other side was tan. He turned it over repeatedly,
observing each side. Then he twirled the paper between
thumb and forefinger and smiled to himself. He twirled
his paper, sucked his thumb furiously, and rocked
himself through this hard time. Chris continued to stroke
himself with that ever-loving frog. Finally, when Polly
returned to feed Chris, the frog dropped free, and Wayne
pounced on it like a spider on a struggling fly. The look of
delight on his face was unmistakable. He now had his
great source of joy back, and he was going to enjoy
himself while it was there.

I saw Wayne approach Chris on other occasions
when Chris was crying and offer up the frog. During his
vigils, Wayne would sit with his thumb in his mouth,
often twirling with rapt fascination a scrap of paper or
colorful cloth. In this way, he toughed out the long
minutes Chris took to gain control of his irascible temper.

It wouldn't be accurate to say that Wayne was
trying to be generous. Wayne doesn't try to be anything.
He just does what he does.

The more we got to know Wayne, the more Polly's
and my views about him converged a good bit. The label
Down's syndrome meant one very important thing to Dr.
Hampster—the child should be institutionalized. But to
us, the label was relatively useless. As his parents we
were only interested in what he *could* do! His limits were
narrower than the other children's, but we didn't need a
label to tell us that. Some people told us that the label
meant Wayne would never walk, or talk, or interact
socially. But we had now come to the point where there
was only one person who could tell us what Wayne was
capable of doing—Wayne himself. And when he got
glasses, he became more responsive not only to the

objects in his environment, but to the people in his environment also. Now Polly had learned to relax a bit when people talked about Wayne's "condition," and she spoke of him as a very different kind of child.

Late one night, when Polly and I were talking, Polly said that she hoped Wayne would die before us. She said he got along by himself in so many ways, but that he really needed a momma and poppa to manage his life. She hoped that he would never have to face life without being provided with his basic needs. I thought of Dr. Hampster, who said that such care and attention were a waste, and for just an instant, I knew clearly in my mind the difference between an objective view and an incomplete view. Just a matter of values, I muttered to myself, and I had to agree with Polly. I, too, wanted Wayne to have his basic needs met in our home, rather than provided by the legions of care-givers in an institution. In this regard, Wayne was no different than any of us; he needed to be with people who loved him.

I think Barney understood this about Wayne all along. We hadn't seen Barney for a while; both of us had been busy. But Barney finally came over shortly after Chris's first birthday, bringing the traditional Cracker Jacks and brew.

Earl, now finishing his senior year in high school, disdainfully took his box and asked Barney some questions about medical school. The more Barney talked, the more Earl was convinced that law would be his field. Mila and Terry came up to him, giggling at a private joke. Terry had a cold, and Barney automatically put his hand on her forehead. "Slight fever," he said and handed her a box of Jacks. Wayne found his box and whooped it up as he headed for his hide-out behind the couch where none of the littler children could come and take advantage of him while he feasted.

Barney paid his respects to Polly and checked out Chris. Chris met his approval, and Barney slid toward my room where I set up the chessboard, and we began to play. Not that "my room" was any guarantee to privacy. The kids wandered in and out from time to time, asking us questions, and Polly came in occasionally to make a comment about the children. But my room was still the most peaceful one under the roof, so Barney and I chatted about his career.

He had lately completed half of his psychiatric residency before firmly deciding that it wasn't for him. Barney didn't approve of the current techniques. He wanted to use what he had learned about healing, and he wanted to be an active part of the healing process. He felt that in psychiatry, no one was really sure what the healing process was or whether psychiatrists were healers or hinderers. But general practice—there it was for Barney! The old family doctor. Settle down in a small town or at the edge of a city and get to know your clientele. Get to know the momma and daddy and observe them as they plant their family tree and branch out. Barney could get into that idea, learning more fully about relationships between people, about birth, growth, and death, and what role, if any, the art of healing played in people's lives. That made sense to Barney. So at thirty-two he resigned from psychiatric residency and took up residency in general medicine.

As we sat at the table, mulling over the chess pieces, the sounds of the house told the story of the day. We could hear Terry and Mila arguing over a mutual friend. Though I couldn't hear the exact words, it was clear one was pulling for the friend, the other against her. Then Earl complained that the girls were making so much noise he couldn't study. Polly called for silence but her request was heeded for only a few moments. The sniping started up again, rekindled by Earl's loud insistence for quiet. In the other part of the house, Chris woke up and screamed for his dinner. Polly got him and went into the kitchen to feed him. I could hear the twins follow her, complaining that they, too, wanted something to eat. Eric was there first, and he teased the twins, who set up a howl, while Earl tried to shout them into silence from his bedroom.

"Your move," I said to Barney.

He looked up. "Yeah, I know."

Through the doorway staggered Wayne. He was exploring, and when he saw us, he toddled over to observe. He started to say something, and I silenced him by putting my finger over my mouth. He did likewise and said, "Shuush!" He stood by me, his arm touching mine, and observed our game like a sage who had spotted the best move but was refusing to divulge it.

In the background I heard Earl, in total
exasperation, slide back his chair, go into the next room
where the girls were, and demand silence. The girls told
him flatly that it wasn't *his* house. The next moment they
were all standing in my doorway, calling for instant
justice from you-know-who, who didn't have any idea
how it all started.

"Earl, why don't you read in here where you won't
be disturbed? Girls, how 'bout going back and trying to
get along—*quietly*," I whispered.

"Little sisters are a drag," Mila said.

"Big sisters are pompous," Terry retorted as the
girls disappeared.

Barney looked up from the board. "What do you
think of your residency?"

"I've gotten used to the sight of blood," I said.
"Really. But a surgeon I ain't. Four hours in the E.R. and
I'm a shambles. I could get into something like
hematology where there isn't all that hacking and
sawing."

"Spoken like a true researcher," Barney said.
"How's that coming?"

"Hematology is the hottest thing in medicine until
you try to get some money to do it."

Polly appeared in the door. "Can you get Eric to
stop picking on the twins?" she asked.

The twins staged a shrill crying to assist me
in my deliberations over the problem. Not to be
out-maneuvered, Eric began running down reasons why
it was he, Eric the Innocent, who had been wronged. I
said something to the boys and they scattered in all
directions, forgetting whatever had caused the problem.
Wayne remained in the room. He went over to Polly and
pulled at her skirt.

"Tea," he said.

Polly ran a hand through his hair. "You ask nicely,
Wayne," she said. "Then you can have tea."

"Pease. Tea." Wayne trudged happily after her.

Barney sat motionless, observing the board. The
sound of footsteps pounded through the house,
punctuated by shrieks as someone got caught. Barney
apparently hadn't been disturbed. He moved his bishop,
thwarting my plans for a quick victory. Earl, however,

had clearly heard the chase and other noises emanating from all over the house. He stood up impatiently and walked around our table.

"Dad," he said, glancing at the board, "you're still developing your knights too quickly and your bishops insufficiently." He continued to pace around the room. "Do you think all families are as noisy as we are, Dr. Newton?"

"Those that have people in them," Barney answered dryly.

Earl sighed heavily and circled back to his books. He shifted his fanny in his chair and struggled with limited success to get into his reading.

I tried in vain to exclude the background noises from my thinking. I had to figure out a way to neutralize Barney's bishop. Frustrated, I got up and went into the kitchen for some snacks. Wayne followed me with his now empty cup in his two hands.

"Pease, m'tea!"

Polly poured the last of the tea into Wayne's cup. Chris fussed for more milk. The twins pulled at Polly's skirts and howled for "ups," then sat upon one another, for reasons unknown to me. Eric went into the girls' room, where their shouts of protest indicated his presence was clearly unwanted, and Wayne sat in the middle of the kitchen, smiling over his tea.

Barney walked in and we watched as Eric got a tablespoon and began a drum beat on Chris's stomach. Markel toddled over and stuck his finger toward Chris's eye, and Michael was not far behind. Just then Wayne stepped over by Chris and said something to the other boys I couldn't understand. But Eric and the twins apparently did, because Eric dropped the spoon and gently touched Chris while Markel and Mike stood back. Chris was crying lustily by this time, and Polly came bursting into the room, alert to anyone who might be doing her youngest any harm. My eyes restrained her, and we stood back and watched.

Eric picked up the spoon and eyed Chris's head with considerable purpose. But again, Wayne said something to Eric, and Eric apparently forgot the spoon treatment, walked over to Chris, and patted him on the head. Wayne kissed Chris, hugged Eric, and walked unsteadily across the kitchen floor, grinning from ear to ear. He went over to Mike, hugged him and kissed him a terrible, slobbery "Wayne special." Then he tottered on to the next recipient.

"What's with Wayne?" Barney asked.

"That's just the way Wayne is," I said. "The whole house can be in an uproar and Wayne shines through it all."

Wayne had now gotten to Markel, kissed him on the nose and forehead, and hugged him till Markel's face turned red. Wayne just giggled and waddled on to Barney. He tugged at Barney's pant leg and demanded up. Barney raised him, and Wayne kissed Barney and hugged him, too. Then Wayne cooed and showed he wanted down.

"Thanks, pal," Barney chortled, "I needed that."

Wayne proceeded to the girls' room and pushed his way in. We heard silence for a moment and then a command. "Wayne, let us alone." Then we heard slobbery kisses and Wayne's giggle and the girls saying with strained patience, "There, will that hold you?"

Wayne emerged from their room and headed for the study where Earl was. We all followed Wayne's progress as he made his unsteady course. He disappeared into the room and we heard Earl telling Wayne to get lost. But he underestimated Wayne's persistence, and soon we heard the wet kiss being administered and the grunts from immense hugs and Earl's grumps as he got back to his studies. Wayne finally emerged from the study, smiling more broadly than ever. Wayne loved his kisses, and Wayne loved his hugs.

The household was now reasonably quiet. We could hear the birds chirping outside and the girls quietly whispering in their room. For the first time in what seemed like hours, they were cooperating. The twins and Eric were playing happily together with the silverware in the middle of the floor, and Chris was dozing contentedly in Polly's arms. Peace and quiet! It was incredible! As if he knew his work was complete, Wayne flopped down on his fat little fanny. He stuck his thumb in his mouth and began to suck. Behind those thick glasses his moist, plum eyes sparkled, and he managed a wide grin around the fist that was stuck in his face.

"Y'know," Barney said, "Wayne is sort of a special person." He stopped for a minute to think. "You know who's the first person in your house to come and give me a hug and a kiss?"

Sure, I knew.

"Whether or not I have Cracker Jacks," Barney said, "Wayne is always the first one to come and greet me. It's kind of nice to have ol' Wayne to count on, to always have someone there to let you know you're appreciated."

That's typical of Wayne, I thought. When I come home from a long trip, I may or may not find the other kids at home. I may or may not hear their shrieks of joy at my return. But you-know-who is always there, laughing elatedly and running wide-armed at me. Wayne seems to know he has a place in our family and his own special identity.

A few days after Barney's visit, we were having our usual rowdy lunch. The girls were trying to see which one could put the most grapes in her mouth at one time without crushing any, Eric was watching and trying to mimic them, and the twins, in a double-seated high chair pulled up to the table, were trying to see how much of the mashed potatoes they could put on the wall without having any drip down onto the floor. All the kids were laughing. Wayne was peering out from behind his very thick Coke-bottle-bottom glasses with a mischievous look on his face. He'd stolen the big kids' sandwiches and hidden them under the research paper I had left on the table. The kids discovered the theft with due outrage.

"Who stole my sandwich?" they began, and the howl increased until they noticed Wayne. Then they knew. From Wayne's girth anyone could tell that he loved to eat, and the delight he displayed was giving him away. Earl pounded on the table and glared at Wayne in mock indignation.

"You fat slob!" he kidded. "You garbage can!"

Wayne just giggled.

Terry's sandwich was gone, too. "You, you hippopotamus! You moose!" she shouted.

"Where are the sandwiches?" they all wailed.

Through it all, Wayne screeched happily. When Polly had had enough, she turned to Wayne. "Come on, you big moose. Give everyone back their sandwiches."

Wayne sniggered, then very innocently uncovered the sandwiches. As the kids gulped down their food,

Wayne pierced the air with his squeals of delight.

After the children had ravaged everything that was on the table, they disappeared to their various pursuits and left me with Wayne. I was now into my paper, only half conscious of what was going on.

"Wayne," Polly said, "bring me the milk bottle from the table, please." Wayne smiled impishly, stood perfectly still, and put his nose straight up in the air. Then he quivered a little as if to let Polly know he had heard her, but not the way she wanted him to. He sniffed delicately at the air to tease her.

"Bring me the milk, Wayne," Polly said, impatient with this game. No response. "Please, Wayne, the other boys are too small to lift it. Only you are big enough to pick up the milk and bring it to me." Wayne bowed in acknowledgment of his singular talents.

"Oose," he said, "Oose." I stopped and put down the research paper. Polly struggled to figure out what Wayne was saying.

"What did you say, Wayne?" she asked. Wayne stood erect, throwing his head back.

"Oose."

Then, with sudden inspiration Polly realized what Wayne had said. "Oh," she said, "good heavens! Please bring me the milk, Moose."

A look of triumph crossed Wayne's face as he fetched her the milk.

A little later in the afternoon, Polly was giving vitamins to all the kids. Wayne refused to take his. "Come on, Moose," Polly said. "Take your medicine." Wayne threw back his head, giving the air his funny little sniff.

Polly, as usual, was in a great hurry and wanted the task done. For a moment she stopped and looked at him. Again, inspiration struck her. "Wayne Oden," she said emphatically, "come take your medicine."

Wayne's eyes got big and round and shocked. He threw his head back again. "Oose, Oose," he said.

Polly looked at him evenly. "It's Wayne Oden until you take your medicine." Quickly, Wayne came over, opened his cavernous mouth, and waited for the medicine to drop in. "Thank you, Moose," Polly said.

Moose beamed at this recognition. He had discovered himself, and he was most delighted.

CHAPTER FOUR

I learned about Down's syndrome from several sources.

One of my buddies in the service had a daughter who was called "mongoloid." Mac was a cheerful young kid who used to take a car full of us single guys home with him so we could have a home-cooked meal. We usually stayed all night playing penny-ante poker. When his wife got real big with child we didn't stay so late. Then he got a three-day pass to become a father. He came back full of statistics: His daughter weighed seven pounds and five ounces, measured nineteen and a quarter inches long, slept twenty-two-and-a-half hours the first day of her life, and sucked four-and-a-half ounces of milk in three attempts. We went to Mac's for dinner and a few hands of stud, and everything seemed okay.

But then something happened. Someone said his child was mongoloid. There were no more dinners at his house and no more card games. We heard no more about his daughter. None of us in Mac's outfit knew quite what "mongolism" was, nor what it did to the child. But we could see what it did to Pfc. George McClinton—he withdrew more and more into his own affairs and became too busy to talk with any of us.

Down's syndrome was also presented during my second year in medical school. We were examining the developmental sequence of organisms. Beginning with the fertilization of a single ovum, we learned, the organism's genetic potential is fully determined. This capacity is then realized as the fertilized egg divides through the process of mitosis into two cells, then into four, and so on. Somewhere along the line the cells begin to differentiate into skin, liver, heart, brain, and muscle cells. The process is still full of mystery, but one thing is for certain: If something is wrong with the first cell, the developing human will have serious problems. Down's syndrome isn't something that happens the same way all the time. The chromosomes, the nucleic acid that controls our development, are like strings of pearls that can get mixed up and result in a Down's fetus. However, the outcome isn't the same every time. In fact, some medical authorities include sixty-five symptoms in thirteen categories, any of which may be apparent in a Down's infant. A baby with eight of the symptoms is usually considered a Down's child. One such list of symptoms appears on pages 48 and 49.

Even though I had been exposed to all this information, none of it prepared us for living with Moose. No one ever said that Moose would sound like he was choking in the middle of the night. I can't count the times Polly and I have leaped out of bed and rushed to his crib, thinking he was strangling to death. Because of Moose's chronic runny nose, we learned to put him on his stomach and pin the sheets down tight so that he wouldn't be able to roll over. In that position, Moose's nose would drain, and he as well as Polly and I could get some sleep. No one told us that we would wash more diapers for Moose than any of the other children or that he'd need them a year and a half longer. No one told us we'd have to learn more patience when talking to Moose because it took him longer to understand verbalizations. Nor did anyone tell us that he would be more sensitive to the tone of our voices than the other children. No one said we'd have to be especially careful to keep Moose away from the stove when we were cooking. Moose did not understand danger and was capable of pulling boiling water or sizzling oil down on himself even at the age of seven.

So when people ask me, "What do you know about Down's syndrome?" I wonder where to begin.

When Dr. Sibyl Sanders, a resident in pediatrics at the Torrance Hospital, asked me to attend a conference with a couple who had had a Down's child, I was sure I knew as much about Down's as anyone she could consult. But I was still trying to pull what I should say out of my mind. I remembered Pfc. McClinton and what the information had done to him. I remembered that call from Dr. Hampster and what Polly and I had been through with Moose. I had vowed that if I ever got the chance to talk to a parent of a new Down's child, I'd improve a great deal on Hampster's performance. But now I was about to face that situation, and my mind was blank.

Sibyl put her arms around my neck and kissed me as soon as she saw me. "Chet, you're looking great," she said. It had been a year—was it two?—no, three years since we'd been interns together.

"Hey, the Wonder Girl has become a Wonder Woman," I said, recalling some old jokes. I had teased her that if she didn't give up the pigtails and blue jeans when she became a doctor, the patients would think she was the doctor's daughter. In white coat and red jersey, she still looked young and too fragile to have been through the emergency scenes we'd handled together at L.A. County General.

"What's up?" I asked.

She smiled and the room lit up. "You know me," she said. "I'm in pediatrics because I can't stand adults!" We both laughed. "I like to help children grow up to be healthy," she added. Then, "I hear you support a pediatrician all by yourself."

I laughed at the reference to my ever-expanding family.

"Well," she continued, "the couple coming in today has a two-week-old son, and I've confirmed a Down's syndrome diagnosis. How do I turn that into good news?"

"Sibyl-of-the-easy-questions," I teased. "Seriously, you can only supply information. What they do with it is up to them."

Sibyl looked at me. "What information? What facts?"

Now I understood why I was here. Sibyl had heard the same lectures in medical school I had heard. She'd read the same books and was probably aware of the same myths.

48

Head	per cent of Down's children showing symptoms

A. Skull
1. Open fontanel beyond 1½ years (soft spot on skull)   16
2. Open sutures (openings on skull)   4
3. Flat occiput (flat back of head)   82

B. Face
1. Wrinkled forehead   14
2. Red cheeks   66
3. Rough and scaly cheeks   74

C. Eyes
1. Slanting eyes   88
2. Epicanthus (vertical fold of skin on eyelid near either side of nose)   50
3. Blepharitis (inflammation of the eyelids)   38
4. Strabismus (cross-eyedness)   14
5. Nystagmus (involuntary rapid eye movement)   14
6. Speckling of iris   30
7. Double zone in iris   22

D. Ears
1. Prominent   50
2. Malformed   48
3. Small or absent lobule   80

E. Nose
1. Flat nose   44
2. Small nose   54
3. Flat nasal bridge   62

F. Mouth
1. Constantly open mouth   62
2. Small mouth   32
3. Broad lips   36
4. Irregular lips   28
5. Dry lips   32
6. Fissured lip (vertical crease in lip)   56
7. Small teeth   56
8. Conical lateral incisors (pointed teeth on front sides)   46
9. Irregular alignment (teeth)   68
10. Widely spaced teeth   28
11. Crowded teeth   38
12. Large tongue   30
13. Furrowed tongue   44
14. Protruding tongue   32
15. High-arched palate   74
16. Narrow palate   52
17. Cleft palate   4
18. Raucous voice   54
19. Low-pitched voice   20

Trunk	per cent of Down's children showing symptoms

G. Neck
1. Broad — 50
2. Short — 50

H. Chest
1. Funnel chest (concave chest) — 12
2. Pigeon breast (convex chest) — 14
3. Flat nipples — 56
4. Heart murmur — 28
5. Dorsolumbar kyphosis (hunchback) — 14

I. Abdomen
1. Diastasis recti (muscle separation in abdominal wall) — 76
2. Umbilical hernia (part of intestine protrudes from navel) — 4

J. Genitalia
1. Small penis — 50*
2. Cryptorchism (undescended testes) — 20*
3. Small scrotum — 42*

K. General
1. Acrocyanosis (fingers, ankles, and wrists discolored red or blue) — 28
2. Hyperextensible joints (extreme extension of limbs) — 88
3. Hypotonic muscles (diminished skeletal muscle tone) — 66

L. Hands
1. Short and broad hands — 74
2. Flabby hands — 84
3. Horizontal creases across palms — 48
4. Short fingers — 70
5. Tapering fingers — 52
6. Short fifth finger — 66
7. Curved fifth finger — 68
8. Only one crease in fifth finger — 10

M. Foot
1. Gap between toes one and two — 44
2. Toe three longer than toe two — 0
3. Plantar furrow (groove across foot sole) — 28

*Of males.

Adapted from Clemens E. Benda, *Down's Syndrome; Mongolism and Its Management.* Rev. Ed. (NY: Grune and Stratton, 1969)

Timothy was Mr. and Mrs. Hooley's first child. Mrs. Hooley was thirtyish and plump from recent pregnancy. Mr. Hooley might have looked younger, except that his weathered face and his faded plaid shirt and jeans added years to his appearance. He carried Timothy in large, calloused, oil-stained mechanic's hands, and when he gave Timothy to Dr. Sanders, the child was barely more than a handful. Both parents were subdued, but just behind their constrained expressions were looks of pride and hope.

"How's my little colt?" Mr. Hooley asked, his smile popping through his reserve like crocus through snow.

"Fine and healthy," Sibyl said. She looked at me for help but there was no way I could tell them for her. She was their doctor, and she would have to begin.

"There are some things you should know." Sibyl psyched herself up for the one thing she hated as a doctor more than anything else. "Timothy is just as strong and healthy as he can be." Now both the Hooleys beamed brightly at their son.

That was a bad move, Sibyl, I thought. There's promise of good things to come.

"Please sit down," she said. "There is something else I want to tell you." She became more serious; she was the warm, concerned doctor.

Okay, I thought, that's more like it.

Sibyl showed the parents the characteristic folds on Timothy's eyelids and the creases extending clear across the palms of his hands. She opened Timothy's mouth to show the high-arched palate. Her voice was low and soft and matter-of-fact.

"These characteristics," she said, "form a pattern. It is called Down's syndrome, and it is associated with some serious conditions. Some Down's children don't . . . live to reach adulthood."

The Hooleys stopped and looked at each other. Mr. Hooley seemed to understand what Sibyl was trying to tell them and put his arm around his wife's shoulders. There was a long pause. Mrs. Hooley buried her head in her hands.

"I can give you an idea of what to expect," Sibyl said, shaken by the impact of the news on the Hooleys. "Timothy will not mature intellectually as quickly as normal children. There will be marked limits on what he can do." Now that Sibyl had said her piece, she searched for more words. Doctors seem to learn somewhere that more words will soften the blow, but Sibyl was having difficulty finding them. "But that's just what it means to doctors," she continued. "This is Dr. Oden. He has a son who is a Down's child."

"I'm Chet Oden," I said, sticking out my hand. Mr. Hooley had an immensely strong grip—it was like shaking hands with a sandpaper vise. He smelled mildly of diesel oil, and I assumed he'd come straight from a shop where worn or broken parts are simply replaced by shiny new ones. This must be a helluva meeting to come to.

"My fourth child, Moose, is a Down's child," I said. Their eyes were glued to me. They wanted something magical. But I was no magician. "Look," I said, "my oldest son fought me all the way. I wanted him to play football, but he didn't like it. He's not a jock. For a while I started to get on him, and both he and I were miserable. Fortunately I realized that the disappointment I felt was my problem, not his. He's now discovered other interests, is away at college, and doing just fine."

"Moose is seven. He's my Down's syndrome boy. I don't care if he doesn't play football, and I don't care if he doesn't go to college. He's learning to be himself and I like that. Polly, my wife, is pregnant with our ninth, and I have no plans for him or her either. But whatever that child becomes will be okay with me."

Mr. Hooley looked down at the floor, then up at me. "I own a garage," he said. "I've built up a good business. I was hoping. . . ."

"Sure," I said. "I know the feeling. You may have more children and one of them may take over the business. Or maybe not. One thing for sure. Timothy won't follow in your footsteps, at least not completely. You'll have to let him make his own way."

Mrs. Hooley wiped away her tears. She took her son in her arms and kissed him. "God's ways are mysterious," she said softly.

"My son brings a lot of joy to my family. I'd like you to meet him. Would you come over to my house—it's not far from here—and meet Moose?"

The Hooleys said they would.

When the Hooleys left, Sibyl stopped me for a moment. "Thanks," she said. "I just couldn't have done that alone." I started to poo-poo her remark. "No," she said, "it's true. Down's is different from a broken leg or measles. Most of the disorders I deal with are outside things that happen to the child. Down's *is* the child. And I had difficulty realizing that Timothy is human, not just a cluster of Latin names. I'd like to visit Moose, too, and get to know him."

"Sure," I said.

"How can I thank you?"

Easy, it was lunch time. When we'd first known each other as interns, a thank-you meant two peanut butter sandwiches and an apple. But Sibyl was going to have to spring for a new standard—a thick steak and a green salad.

The Hooleys did come over to visit. Polly looked as if she were carrying a watermelon under her skirt and she waddled under the extra weight. She put the coffee on and began to cut some cake.

"My goodness," Mrs. Hooley said, observing the activity of our eight children. "You must have your hands full!"

"I come from a large family," Polly replied. "It must look like a lot more than it is."

After we served the coffee and cake, you-know-who toddled into the room. "Hi, Moose," I said, "I knew you'd be along to hijack some goodies."

Moose grinned and took a bite of cake off my fork. Then he saw the Hooleys and their child. He walked over to them and pointed to Timothy. "Baa," he said.

Chris was just a year and a half, and he came over too, dragging his blanket behind him. He was a lot shyer than Moose and needed some coaxing. When Timothy was shown to him, Chris looked up at Mrs. Hooley and said, "Baba."

Soon the adults were surrounded by the children's activity. Eric chased the twins around the room and Chris screamed to get in on the fun. With his little two-legged gallop, Moose tried in vain to keep up with the four-year-old twins. Soon Moose tired of the chase and came over by me again. Another bite of cake and off he went to watch Timothy. Mrs. Hooley pulled back

Timothy's blanket and showed him to Moose. Moose clapped his hands and Mr. Hooley swooped Moose onto his knee. When Mr. Hooley bounced him, Moose giggled and bobbed his head with each jolt. After the ride, Moose gave Mr. Hooley's leg a big hug. Each time Mr. Hooley looked at Moose, Moose grinned and bobbed his head.

After a couple of hours, Mrs. Hooley bundled up Timothy and they got ready to go. "Thank you for asking us," she said. She looked a long time at Moose. He came up to her and gave her a kiss.

"Baa," he said, patting Timothy's blanket.

"Yes. Baby," said Mrs. Hooley.

"Please don't let this stop you from having other children," I said.

About six months later we got a simple card from the Hooleys. It said Mrs. Hooley was pregnant and Timothy was doing fine. I called Mr. Hooley at work to congratulate him on the forthcoming birth. "Say," I added, "if you hear about someone having a Down's child, visit them, okay?"

I often thought about the Hooleys and remembered how helpless Sibyl Sanders had felt as their pediatrician. I was very frustrated to be a member of a profession which, until now, had concentrated on describing Down's syndrome in terms of the limits it placed on children. In terms of "can'ts." I don't care what kind of doctor gets the job, telling parents that their newborn will walk late, talk late, and generally develop differently than normal children is a quick way to get depressed.

And it doesn't need to be that way. As I looked at Moose, I wondered at the things he could do that I never expected he would.

Moose was developing traits that none of our other children would acquire. One was an adventuresome spirit . . . or perhaps an independent curiosity. Maybe he was just naturally more gregarious than the rest. Whatever it was, it gave us our share of headaches as well as pleasure.

One late afternoon, I came home and found Polly running down the street calling for Moose at the top of her lungs. Moose had slipped out an open door and taken off on the first of many excursions. Since Polly was going one way, I decided to go the other. I ran three blocks before I found him. A paperboy was sitting on the corner, folding his newspapers, and Moose was sitting beside him.

"Moose, what are you doing?" I accused.

The paperboy came to his defense. "Nothing. He's just sitting here, helping me."

The paperboy was a nice kid who said Moose could help him anytime he wanted to.

For two weeks after that, we were very careful about closing the front and back doors. But then one Saturday morning when Polly and I were enjoying late coffee in the kitchen, we noticed the silence in the house. At once, we both leaped out of our chairs and confirmed our fears—the front door was open! We called in the older children, who were playing in the back yard, but they denied letting Moose out of the house. I went one way to search and Polly went the other, and we met on the far side of the block. No Moose. Discouraged, we trudged back home and decided to call the police.

Just as we walked in the door, the phone rang. It was Joyce Severensen. Calmly, she explained that Moose had walked the two blocks to her house and was at that moment eating cookies with Donny. She said he'd be there when we wanted him. We raced over, expecting him to be in near panic.

But when we came in, Moose looked happily at us and displayed his latest loot—a sugar cookie—which he proceeded to eat.

"Want to come home?" I said.

"No," Moose shook his head. When I picked him up, Moose cried all the way to the door.

Polly and I were too relieved to scold Moose for running away. I wasn't sure he'd understand me even if I did. But when we got him home, we put him in the living room and I watched him for half an hour. He and I played marching to the music on the radio. He liked that and kept a pretty good beat.

Eventually Moose toddled over to the front door and opened it with a couple of raps of his fat little hand. In an instant he was perambulating down the front walk on another of his excursions! When we'd corralled him, I put a hook and eye on the front door and felt pretty sure that Moose would be rendered home bound. And he was for a while. But it seemed the little critter hadn't tasted wanderlust for the last time.

Spring warmed into summer and the big kids played in the sprinklers out in front of the house. I was studying, and Polly was up to her ears in wash. She'd gone to the laundry room for another load and discovered the back door open. She let out a yelp and I jumped, smoking all the way down the hall.

Moose had gone out the back door, and the only open avenue was toward the neighbor south of us, who had a new swimming pool. The pool was fenced in, but the kids often left the gate open, and Polly and I must have had the same thought together. We raced for the pool area and found Moose and Mr. Dohrman, the owner of the pool, standing by the diving board.

"Thank God!" Polly said.

Mr. Dohrman looked up. "You missing someone?"

"Our junior explorer," Polly said, "can't swim."

Mr. Dohrman stroked his chin. "Good instincts. He won't go *near* the water!" We stood around for a moment to see what Moose would do. He made a beeline for the Dohrmans' old Beagle hound, eyeing the pool as he went. The dog sniffed Moose's hand, wagged his tail, and barked.

Moose giggled and clapped his hands. "Woof," he repeated.

I picked Moose up. "I don't like you to run away!" I said as sternly as I could.

"Woof!" Moose said again, and giggled.

"You can use the pool," Dohrman said to me, "but let me know first."

"Sure. And keep the gate closed," I said. "This little Houdini may not get the message."

For a time our watchfulness prevented further escapades. Then David was born. Moose had learned from past experience that when momma was with a new baby, Moose was on his own.

Perhaps the excitement of the new child caused Polly's vigilance toward Moose to relax, as it had with the other babies. At any rate, one day she found the front door open again. A ruler, apparently the device Moose used to unhitch the hook and eye, was lying across the threshold. I was unreachable, so Polly turned the kids loose in search while she circled the block in the car. Mila was the first to find Moose, but everyone else in the neighborhood was in close pursuit.

Moose had somehow opened our neighbor's gate and was now inside poking a branch into their German shepherd's ear. The dog was barking, and Moose was trying to outbark him. Whenever the dog fell silent, Moose jabbed him with the stick until he barked again. Then Moose barked back. It was the din that brought the entire neighborhood to the dog's assistance.

After that incident I installed a chain on our door, but Moose solved that by pushing a chair up to the door and sliding the chain loose. Next, I installed bells on all the doors so at least we'd hear them chiming when he swung them open to make his escapes, but Moose quickly learned to open the doors without making a jingle. Finally, we realized that Moose's increasingly frequent and wide-ranging adventures were really no threat to him. We discovered that the easiest thing to do when Moose disappeared was to relax and wait for the phone to ring. It seemed that everyone in our six-block area knew who Moose was, and they simply called us when he came meandering into their yards or homes.

What I hadn't realized was that Moose did more than just wander the neighborhood. He also communicated his love of peaches. When Moose stepped onto a neighbor's porch or let himself in a front door or back door, he was greeted warmly. Then the inevitable offer: a cookie, a cracker, a glass of milk. Moose would protest, "No! 'Each!'" until they understood he wanted peaches instead. Neighbors began storing a peach or two in their refrigerators in case Moose came over. He had his "rounds" apparently, so he didn't appear at any one person's house too often.

I learned a valuable lesson about Moose through all this. It began after we received a coupon, permitting us to take the local paper at a special rate. The paper carrier came over to make the arrangements.

"Hi, kid," I said. "What's the deal now?"

Moose was tugging at my leg. "D'man," he was saying.

The paperboy explained how the deal worked—one month low cost, and after that the paper was regular. I made it clear I wanted the paper for only one month, and he said fine.

Again, Moose was at my leg. "D'man," he said.

"Okay, pal," I said.

I stuck out my hand to indicate we had a deal, no problems.

"I've seen you around the neighborhood," I said. "What's your name?"

"D'man," Moose said.

"Dohrman," the paperboy said.

Hearing them that close together, I suddenly realized that Moose was saying something pretty close to *Dohrman*. I didn't believe it. I turned to Moose and pointed to the paperboy. "What's his name?" I asked.

"Dayup."

"No, no, *I'm* daddy. Who is *that* boy?"

"Dayup," Moose insisted stubbornly. He started climbing up my leg. "Dayup," he said.

"Okay." I picked Moose up.

"Kid," he said.

I kissed him and he smiled. "Now who is that boy?"

Moose smiled, "D'man!"

I roared into the kitchen where Polly was cleaning up the dinner dishes. "This dude knows the name of the paperboy!" I shouted.

Polly faced me squarely. "Why does that surprise you?" she said.

"Names are hard to remember." I put Moose on my shoulders and walked over to the Dohrmans'. "Who lives here?" I asked Moose.

"D'man," he replied.

We walked down the street toward the Berrys', who owned the German shepherd. "Who lives here?" The dog came up and barked.

"Woof! woof!" Moose said, laughing.

"Who else lives here?"

"Bawwy," he said.

We went down the block and stopped at all the places I could remember that Moose had frequented in his peach raids. One by one, he named them, or at least gave reasonable facsimiles. Finally we came to the Severensens'. "Who lives here?"

"Donny."

"What's his last name?"

"Donny."

"That's his first name," I insisted. "What's his last name?"

"Donny," Moose said with finality.

"Well, you got it sort of right," I conceded. "You do a helluva lot better than I do."

Joyce Severensen came into the yard and waved. "Taking a walk?"

It was a pleasant way to invite conversation. "Hey, I'm testing Moose's memory for names. Did you know this little pirate knows the names of eleven neighbors who've been handing out peaches to him?"

Joyce laughed. "Peaches? He thumps on my door demanding sugar cookies."

By this time Moose had broken free from me and rushed up to Joyce. He stopped in front of her and jumped up and down excitedly. "Waisin, waisin," he pleaded. Donny came out and they rushed up to each other and both started talking at once. Joyce went inside and returned with some sugar cookies with raisins on top. Both boys ran for her, nearly knocking her down. Donny snatched his cookie and ran around her in circles. But before she gave Moose his cookie, she squatted down to his level. Moose threw his arms around her neck and gave her a big hug and kiss. Then he took his cookie and added a bonus kiss.

"I don't know what it is," she laughed, "whether he just likes my cookies, or hates my peaches!"

CHAPTER FIVE

In the late 1960's, when Moose was eight, we began exploring our community for public schools which would open their doors to him. I believed that there were some pretty fundamental things that Moose needed to learn at home, but I also thought that school should serve as more than just a day-care center for him. I looked to school to help Moose extend his experience, to provide a place where he could learn about other people, and to help him acquire the skills of modern living.

We had looked up the available schools in the local directory and had asked, word-of-mouth, for others. The complete list wasn't very long to begin with, and we knew that some schools had special criteria for eligibility. Polly visited them, one by one, and underwent the interviews to see if Moose was eligible. She soon felt somewhat discouraged by the same litany of questions.

"Come in, Mrs. Oden. This must be Wayne!"

"I'm Moose."

"I have a few questions I'd like you to answer, Mrs. Oden. They shouldn't be very difficult for you. First of all, is Wayne toilet trained?"

Polly always answered dutifully, "Yes, since he was three. He has had a few accidents, but only when he was tired or excited."

"Of course. But we won't get tired here or overly excited, will we, Wayne?"

"Moose," Moose would insist.

"Can he be left alone with other children?"

"We have both younger and older children in the house," Polly would smile, understating the case, "and

Moose is very good with all of them. Moose loves people."

The interviewer would look up, as if to see Moose for the first time. "Good! It's so easy for children to hurt each other. And does he feed himself?"

"Oh yes, but he needs to have his meat cut into pieces for him. He can't use a knife very well and that frustrates him."

A few notes. An approving smile. "Does Wayne follow simple directions?"

"Yes, he can follow directions. But there are times when he's a little stubborn, just like all children."

"Naturally. There's so much to learn. We'll contact you when we've made our decision, Mrs. Oden. There are many children needing special classes, as you probably know, and few schools offer special programs. It was nice talking with you, Mrs. Oden, and you, too, Way . . . er, Moose. Nice meeting you, too."

Moose would radiate his approval.

After Polly interviewed all the schools we could find, the second step in the selection process began. First, she scratched off a number of schools because they were really little more than baby-sitting operations with rather punitive management philosophies. She crossed off a few more that were co-ops which had little or no professional staff. From the remaining names on the list, Polly selected those we felt had at least some promise of providing Moose with useful experience. She called five.

Apparently it was fairly standard for the schools to ask several parents and their children to come at the same time for "observation." The children were put in a room equipped with all sorts of toys, while the school counselor and/or school administrator chatted with the parents about the children's behavior. They frowned, for example, if children threw blocks at each other or ran screaming for other children; and they didn't especially like youngsters biting big chunks out of anyone, whether it was teacher or fellow student. Small chunks . . . well, nobody's perfect. But this was a silly test for ol' Moose. You know what Moose did for thirty minutes? He kissed all the girls (and only some of them cried). He hugged everyone and danced around on his tippy toes when they played some music. Moose knew how to gain the keys to any old school he wanted to.

So mother and child were two of the sources of information that schools used to screen prospective students. The other source, as far as I could tell, was the intuition of the head supervisor, a little voice flashing green for admit, and red for reject. I really don't know if the lights were hooked up to anything, if hard evidence was used in their decisions, but most teachers had rather positive vibes about Moose. After the grueling selection process, he was invited to attend four of the five schools which met our criteria. Moose was ready for his first shot at formal education.

South Bay School for Slow Learners was a state operated school partially funded with federal monies. It was associated with a Headstart project and designed for children like Moose, who wouldn't be capable of handling regular sessions or even enriched regular classrooms. It was intended for students who were capable of learning and becoming more useful citizens, the "trainable mentally retarded." TMR was a new concept, and we hoped that the recent M.A. graduates from the University of California School of Special Education who were hired to staff the school would offer Moose as good an experience as possible. As I look back on it, it may have been the other way around.

At about this time, the nation's conscience was just beginning to accept the right of women to take an equal place in society. And Ms. Taylor, Moose's teacher, was the first person I'd met to use the title "Ms." I was unused to the title, but Moose took her at her word and handled it without any problems.

Take your basic question to Moose after three days of school.

"How do you like your teacher, Moose?"

"Goo. Goo. Haw bed in sky. Pay boy-girl."

"Hmmmm. What's her name?"

"Miz Tayloh."

"Oh! Is that Miss or Mrs. Taylor?"

"Miz Tayloh," with rising irritation.

I got down on my haunches so he could see my mouth make the sounds. "Is it Misss or Misssesss Taylor?"

Moose stomped his foot indignantly. He'd said it correctly, and he was going to insist on recognition for this accomplishment. That's how she'd said it, and that's how he was going to repeat it. "Mizzz Tayloh," he bellowed.

"Oh, I see, Moose. Ms. Taylor."

We guessed that Ms. Taylor's methods were a little eccentric, judging from repeated mention of "hot bread in sky" and "playing boy-girl." So when we received a note from her after about two weeks, suggesting we get acquainted, our curiosity was sufficiently aroused. Polly had hassled to find the school, and she was now very big with (soon to be) Aaron, so I decided to take some time to see what this was all about.

I think the best way to see how a school operates is to arrive when you aren't expected. So I left an hour earlier than the appointment, and when I got to Moose's room I began to understand Moose's messages. The tables were pulled together to form a sort of platform in the middle of the room, and sitting in the chairs on top of them, were the children and a young woman, apparently Ms. Taylor. The boys and girls were talking and stuffing pieces of fresh bread into their mouths while Ms. Taylor busily tore off more chunks, buttered them, and passed them around.

I stood in the doorway and called out loudly enough for her to hear. She spotted me and waved for me to come in. She quickly tore off a huge chunk of bread, buttered it, and held it down to me. (When you come to visit someone in a war, you don't take what they have to offer. It might be poisoned. But when you come in peace, you gotta take that chance.) I accepted the bread, which was still warm and smelled, rather than tasted, good.

Ms. Taylor looked at her watch and jumped up. "Good heavens, look what time it's getting to be!" she exclaimed. "If you want to, you can help me get the children down."

I started helping kids down. "Y'know," I said as we unloaded the stage and began to rearrange the tables and chairs, "I don't know about the other children up there, but Moose is about as stable as a sailor on stilts. And," I added, "he has terrible vision. If, for any reason, his glasses fell off, he'd be helpless and in danger up there."

Ms. Taylor exhibited an open smile that showed no hard feelings. She moved in a carefree way, tossing her long chestnut hair over her shoulders. "Boys and girls

need to be free," she said easily, "Moose most of all. But
if you don't want him up here, he can eat his bread with
his chair on the floor. Children only fall when they are
frightened of something," she went on, "but you didn't
come here to hear me prattle on." She paused.

"As a matter of fact," I said, "it was you who
called me."

She raised her hand in front of her face like a
blade, and chopped down, in a sort of impatient gesture.
"Oh yes! The office called and we're meeting each parent
this week!" It was the second time she used that little
gesture to show impatience with herself. "Excuse me a
moment, please." She turned to the class. "Okay,
children," she said in a calm voice, "let's pair off. A boy
and girl at each table. You know where to go." She
waited for a few moments and directed children to their
positions. "Now get out your dolls," she said sweetly.

There was a rustle of activity, and she helped a few
children locate their plastic dolls. Each girl's doll wore a
dress, and each boy's doll wore trousers. Although there
were two blacks in the class of fourteen, Moose and
another little boy who appeared normal, all the dolls were
white, or to be more picky, yellowish-pink.

"Now remember, boys and girls," Ms. Taylor
instructed, "you want to get your dolls talking together.
And we know that dolls can't really talk, so you'll have to
do their talking and acting for them."

Some of the boys and girls began helping their
dolls talk, and Ms. Taylor nodded her approval. Then she
turned to me. "What do you think of our little
home-away-from-home?"

I shook my head. "Hey, Ms. Taylor. I don't know.
I can't even guess what you are up to."

"I try to give the children what they need," she
said warmly. "Like in our cafe in the sky, I try to give
them the security of home, the feeling that their wants
and fantasies are worthwhile and that they should believe
in themselves."

All that from sitting precariously on a table top? I
wondered. I really didn't know much about theories of
education, but this one sounded a bit harebrained to me.

"And this doll-role-playing. It's just what the boys
and girls need." She continued to smile ingenuously.
"They need practice in expressing themselves, in

communicating to another person what they are feeling. I sense that many of them are frustrated because people supply words for them or tell them what they should be feeling without giving them a chance to express themselves."

"How do you determine what a boy or girl needs?" I asked innocently. And that's how she answered.

"You can just *tell*," she said. She cocked her head and contemplated me. "I mean, *I* can just . . . I don't know . . . just *feel* it. Can't you?"

Suddenly I felt very cynical. "No." It was a direct answer, but it seemed inadequate.

"Of course, I've had a lot of training," she added. "But then, as I think about it, I didn't learn *that* from any formal schooling. You either feel it, or you don't."

I looked evenly at her. "How do you know whether or not you're asking the children to do the right thing?"

"Oh," she laughed, "you just watch the children. They'll tell you. I don't mean in words, but in their actions."

I looked around the room. Some children were playing with the dolls, others weren't. Moose and his girl playmate had their dolls laying down, and they were feeding them. "I have a sudden, intuitive feeling that if I asked, Moose would tell me the doll's name was David," I said, half seriously.

Ms. Taylor clapped her hands. "See how simple it is?" She called across the room to Moose, and you know his answer. "See," she prompted, "how easy it is to trust your intuition?"

I had that one coming. But still, I was trying to understand Ms. Taylor, not become one of her disciples. "Why does Moose play with a white doll?"

She frowned, her smile disappearing for the first time since we'd met. "The sets only come in white," she said, and I wanted to kiss her for recognizing the racial problem.

"You could paint them," I suggested, "or get other sets."

"Paint them!" Ms. Taylor was delighted at the idea. "We'll do that tomorrow! Each child can pick a color he or she likes, and they can all paint their dolls." Good Lord, I thought, how did I get into this?

"But how do you know if the role-play *works*?"

"Oh, I look," she insisted. "Just let your eyes see what's happening! Look at Moose. You can just *tell* he's working out his conflicts about his baby brother! That's the hardest part of growing up!"

I looked at Moose. My eyes told me he was doing just what he'd be doing if he were at home. I didn't see any unwinding of tensions. "Ms. Taylor," I began, "I don't see that Moose is getting anything out of this. Really! Maybe you could tell me what to look for!"

If I was expecting to get an argument, I was about to be surprised right out of my socks. "Oh, dear!" she said. "And you have such good intuitions about Moose! We'd better stop this now, and get into something that meets the children's needs. Do you think we should take the children out for recess?"

I shrugged. "Don't you do that on schedule?"

"Of course," she smiled. Then suddenly she stopped and looked at her watch. "Oh my," she said. "I've got to call my husband. You stay here with the children and do what you feel they need. I'll be right back." And with that she ran out of the room.

"Ms. Taylor!" I called after her. But she had disappeared through the door and I was left with the children. To do what was best for them. I considered leaving the room, too. No, that would have been best for *me*, but probably not for them.

I went over to Moose and sat beside him. As I put my weight on his table, it groaned painfully. "Shh," Moose said, "Dabid seeping."

"Yeah," I whispered, "you have him tucked in nicely. What's your friend's name?"

Moose grinned broadly and put his arm around her. He almost took her head off in his display of affection. "Issa," he said, and tightened his grip on her in his enthusiasm.

"Moose!" I said, "ease up on her, or you won't have a friend. Now her name is Lisa, right?"

"Issa," he said decidedly.

"Elizabeth," I offered, trying to capture what he was saying.

"Issa," he said impatiently, pronouncing it exactly as he had the two previous times.

It's amazing how dense a father can be. "Lizzy?"

Moose was turning a darker color. "Issa!" he shouted.

I turned to Issa and asked, "What's your name?"

"Ahy," she said, just barely managing a smile through her fear of me. Moose and I had been hollering at each other at a volume required in our house where there were usually three other conversations going on in addition to the TV.

"Hey," I said, "easy. I don't bite!" I could really get into what she must be feeling, with this giant black bear hovering over her like a mountain about to have an avalanche. I sat down on the floor so she could look straight across at me.

"I'm Chet," I said softly and wondered how silly I would look if anyone stepped into the room and observed us. "What is your name?"

Issa cowered away from me. Fright was still in her eyes. "Ahy," she repeated inarticulately.

Up came Moose. He put his arm around her. "Daddy," he said, pointing to me. "At's my daddy." He plopped himself in my lap and began tickling me until I started to laugh. Then Issa very slowly, very carefully, took a step forward and stopped, waiting to see if I was going to leap upon her. When I did nothing but laugh at Moose's tickling, she took another step. Soon she was sitting on my lap and laughing also. Then she tentatively put her finger out toward my face. I smiled and remained very still now. She touched my cheek, then looked at her finger.

"No, Issa, it won't come off," I said.

Apparently, some of the other children had been watching us. Soon, another boy came up and stared at me. It was as if he was asking permission to join the game. Moose looked at him and said again, "My daddy!" and the little boy plopped himself down on my lap. In a few moments, there were a dozen children sitting all over me. Some were rubbing my face, others had their fingers in my hair, and still others were peering in my ears.

It was then that Ms. Taylor decided to return. "Oh," she said, delighted, "I see you're into trust building."

I disentangled myself from the children and went to her. "Honestly," I said, "I don't understand the cafe in the sky, or the boy-girl game, or trust building. May be great if the experts say so. But you know what? I can't understand what these kids are saying at *all*! I hope you won't take it as meddling in your affairs, but it would certainly be a service to each child here and to those who have to talk with the children, if you'd just help them speak their names more clearly!"

Smile. Exuberance. "Of course. What a super idea! You have such a feel for these children. Have you ever thought of going into special education?"

"Only once," I said jokingly, "so I took two aspirin and went to bed. Say, what is that little girl's name?" I asked, referring to Issa.

Ms. Taylor responded. "Melissa."

Of course. I should have known. "And you call her 'Lissa'."

Ms. Taylor knitted her brow at me in mild disapproval. "You knew all along."

"Not really," I said, "but I should have."

"Well," Ms. Taylor said, winding it up, "I will begin teaching the children how to speak more clearly. Please feel free to drop in. Any time. Okay? I'd like to meet your wife someday," she added. "You must have an interesting family. Moose is always talking about you."

"Sure," I said, trying to imagine how she understood what Moose said. "Why don't you drop over to the house sometime after school or on the weekend."

As I went to my car, I began to give Moose a little more credit. He knew exactly what he was saying when he described the activities in Ms. Taylor's class.

In a couple of weeks, I went back to Ms. Taylor's classroom. I half expected to see the kids sitting up there on their tables when I arrived. But I was wrong. In fact, there were no tables and chairs in the room. Rather, the furniture was outside the classroom in a tangled mess. Inside, the children were sitting in swings, basket affairs suspended from the ceiling by long pieces of nylon rope. They were all laughing and shouting and licking candy canes.

"Not candy canes," Ms. Taylor corrected me. "They are taste sticks." She went to her desk and pulled out several pencil-shaped objects in translucent red, orange, and yellow. "Here," she said, sticking the red one in my face, "taste this."

"Hey," I said, "that's hot!"

"Cinnamon," she said, "to be precise. Now try this one."

The yellow one was sour. "Lemon, in the name of accuracy," she corrected me again. "Children need to know about their world of tastes. They need to have labels for things that taste different.

"We adults take so much for granted. Little children, especially our little children, have so much to learn. We just can't take things for granted."

I gave Moose a lick of my candy . . . er, I mean taste stick. "Cinnamon," I said.

Moose scowled deeply. "No!" he exclaimed. "Shop!"

I agreed that it tasted pretty sharp, alright. Moose went to get his lunch bucket. He opened it up, and took out a plastic container. He opened the container and displayed a baked pear. Lacing the pear was a brownish sauce. "At si'mon!" he said.

I hung around for the language lesson, figuring I'd earned the right to observe by helping Ms. Taylor take down the swings and carry in the table and chairs.

Up to now, I'd thought Ms. Taylor was a bit dizzy. But then I watched her work with the class. She broke the children into three groups. Two of them she set up in the corners of the room around tables. She gave each group a tape recorder which she turned on. Each group was to follow the recording and copy the sounds it made. Soon the room was a barnyard of cackles, moos, and bleats, as the children echoed the sounds on the recorder. Ms. Taylor worked with each child in the remaining group.

"My name is . . ." she said and looked up. The children looked back at her. "Repeat after me, my name is. . . ."

Moose was the first to respond. "Miz Tayloh!"

Ms. Taylor smiled and told him he was a smart boy. Then she asked them to play copycat. She stood, and all the children stood. Then she sat, and they followed suit. Then she said, "My name is . . ." and the children said, "My name is . . ."

Ms. Taylor clapped her hands and looked up to me, to be sure I'd noticed their success.

Soon she had each student standing and saying his or her name.

"My name is Moose Oden," said Moose.

"Moose is your nickname. Your whole name is Chester Wayne Oden."

Moose tried hard to mimic her, but his speech machinery wasn't as mobile or well controlled as hers, and he continued to struggle unsuccessfully for several minutes. Ms. Taylor sensed that he was at his limit and went on to the next student.

The method looked reasonably successful to me. She was very patient and seemed able to get sounds out of the kids that I didn't think they had in them.

Watching them, it struck me that Moose wasn't an isolated accident of nature. Rather, he was one of many like himself. I suddenly felt strange, like I had been luckier than I realized. There are so many things that can go wrong with a person: eyes, ears, brain, endocrine system, bones, muscles . . . my god, the body is complicated. What a miracle it is for anyone—for me—to come out with a sound body!

As I watched Moose and his pals struggling to pronounce words their younger brothers and sisters had mastered long before, I felt a sudden hunger in my guts. All along I'd been escaping to laboratories where I could stay away from people and the frustrations they caused me. The knot within me told me I'd been wrong. I belonged with people. I needed to be involved with them, especially with those who weren't as lucky as others.

Moose moved to one of the groups who were listening to the tape recorder. As he received the first sounds, he acted out the part of the animal. Then his neighbors also began acting out the sounds and adding their own sounds. A parade spontaneously formed as the children began tooting and chugging around the room, oblivious that they were disturbing others. Their vocalizations had reverted back to noises they already knew how to produce; they had abandoned attempts to learn new sounds. I looked at Ms. Taylor, who directed her gaze back to the rebels. She smiled reassuringly at me and went back to her work. Now the other group began to get restless, too.

"Moose," I called, "back to the table." Moose stopped in his tracks and looked up. He grinned broadly. Then he stood up stiff as a rail, put his face to the heavens, and gave a high, piercing laugh. He'd had his fun. Now he went back to the desk and began again imitating the sounds of the recorder.

After the bell dismissed the children for recess, I approached Ms. Taylor. "Don't you ever discipline the children?" I asked.

She frowned. "Sometimes. But they usually know what they need."

"Then you must be upset that I stopped Moose from playing and sent him back to his task."

She put her hand comfortingly on my arm. "Oh, don't feel that way! I don't mind at all. You have such good intuition!"

I looked at her, wondering if she really believed that. I frowned. "Do you have children?" I asked.

"Oh, yes," she beamed, "Randy. He's eight. Or is it nine?"

"A boy! Where does he go to school?"

"But then," she said, still on the last question, "he isn't actually my son . . . he just likes to ride horses, and so do I."

I wanted to ask Ms. Taylor what day it was. I suspect she would have told me it was Wednesday here and now . . . but then, it might be Thursday somewhere else. . . .

Don't get me wrong. I didn't dislike Ms. Taylor. In fact, I have to admit I was sort of fascinated by her.

When I told Polly about Ms. Taylor's class, she didn't believe me, so I invited Ms. Taylor over to the house for lunch one weekend. She came, bringing Randy, and explained to Polly about intuition and children's needs. Polly was a bit bewildered by the explanation just as I'd been, but we all enjoyed one another, and she and Randy visited often after that.

Ms. Taylor had a strange effect on Moose. When she came into the house, he would sing out with laughter and run about like a colt gone berserk. He would throw things and skid on his tummy across the kitchen floor. He'd hug everyone's legs and dance with his brothers, things he'd never even consider doing at any other time.

Every time Ms. Taylor left the house I had to throw a net over Moose and settle him down for half an hour afterward. Then the household would return to normal. And every time she left, Polly got sort of embarrassed. "I don't remember her name," Polly would say. "Is it Miss Tyler, or Mrs. Railer?"

I'd chuckle to myself. It was nice to know that it wasn't just Moose and me. "Something like that," I'd say reassuringly, "something like that."

CHAPTER SIX

The feeling I'd had while watching Moose and his fellow students struggle to learn the simple lessons his teacher tried to teach them returned to me time after time during the next two years. I'd become a medical researcher—my longtime goal—and while this was satisfying in many respects, I felt there was still something missing in my life.

By now our son Aaron was a year old, and with the birth of Brett, Polly and I thought of the Oden family-building as complete. "Brett," we said when we came home from the hospital, "you are forever the baby of the Odens." He didn't really seem to mind.

We had a lot to be thankful for. The oldest children were doing well in college and the others were thriving at home. We were happy and settled in our California home.

Then, out of the blue, my Aunt Ruth called to tell me that my father had died while duck hunting with a friend up in the Red Lake area of Minnesota. They had settled in a marshy lowland that was covered with early ice and a heavy snow. Dad's dog was having trouble in a tangle of reeds, and when Dad went to help him, he broke through the thin ice into about six feet of water. As Aunt Ruth talked, my imagination filled in the picture. Then she asked if I would come back home and help settle Dad's business interests, a small chain of restaurants in Minneapolis and St. Paul.

I said yes, packed up what belongings were worth the effort, and put them on top of our station wagon. I resigned my research position, bade friends goodbye, and jammed Odens into the Chevy until I thought the tires would pop.

My father's estate provided a few bucks, and with it I bought an eleven-acre farm on the east side of St. Paul, about thirty minutes from the university. The boys could have a big dog, we could have a few horses and some cattle, and we'd have a large garden and plenty of space between us and our nearest neighbor, a luxury we'd almost forgotten in California. The extra room proved to be a wise move, and permitted us to expand in a way I'd never imagined when we bought the place.

Suddenly my life seemed to be up in the air. As I look back, I almost believe I was looking for a chance, an excuse maybe, to hang up research and reconsider what I wanted to do with my life. Managing rib joints didn't exactly fall like a blessing from heaven—I knew I wouldn't stay in the business long—but working there gave me time to think.

I'd been tending to business interests for several weeks when I met three black youths who'd worked for Dad part-time, handling the meat orders and other supplies. Meeting them reaffirmed my desire to work with people, especially those who were "underdogs."

The boys were receiving an order of ribs at one of the restaurants, and I was there when the big semi backed up to the thick doors housing the walk-in meat cooler.

They were good looking, clean-cut young kids, joking among themselves as they guided the truck back towards the cooler. I watched them unload the large crates of fresh ribs, weigh each crate, and carefully record the weight before stacking it on the shelf. While they were finishing up the unloading, I went to the office and waited. Soon they came puffing in, smiles on their faces. Each boy brought in a piece of paper with an awkwardly scrawled column of numbers on it and a total at the bottom.

"What's that?" I asked.

The tallest boy stepped forward. "That's the weight of the crates, sir." He pointed to the bottom figure. "That's the total. You can check my figures, but I think they're right," he said.

"Is that the tare weight, or the net weight?" I asked.

He looked at me uncertainly. "That's the weight weight," he said, trying to answer my question.

Okay, I told myself. I learned one set of terms; they're using another set. I thought a moment. Then I asked, "What's your name?"

The tall boy shifted uncomfortably. "Er, ah, Tyrus. You can check my adding . . ."

"Tyrus," I said, "if I went out there in the cooler, and took the meat out of the crates and weighed it, I'd get a certain weight. If I weighed just the wooden crates the meat came in, I'd get a different weight. Right?"

Tyrus looked at me. He shook his head and checked with his pals. They didn't have any better idea than he what I was raving about.

I backed up. A vague suspicion was beginning to take form. "Tyrus, tell me. Did you weigh the meat plus the crates or just the meat without the crates?"

Tyrus smiled. It was a warm, genuine smile. "Both, sir," he said, now sure of what was expected of him. "We always weigh them, crate and all."

"Okay, guys," I said, "listen up. Suppose this was your restaurant. Suppose you paid a dollar and a half a pound for meat. Your delivery man piles your meat on the scale, then sits on the scale himself, and charges you for the total weight."

"Rip off!" said Tyrus. "I'd get me a new delivery man!"

"Good," I sighed, feeling I'd passed the first hurdle. "Now those wooden crates are just like the delivery man sitting on the scale. I don't want to pay a dollar and a half a pound for wooden crates."

"Hey," they agreed, "right on!" Without another word, they raced out of my office and into the cooler. In twenty minutes they came back in. "You know there's thirty-five pounds of crates there," Tyrus said.

I smiled. "Hey, man, you just got the tare weight. Now subtract that from the gross weight and you get the net weight! See, you've just saved me about fifty-two bucks!"

They looked proudly at each other. I was sure I'd never have to remind them about that again. "Okay," I said. "Now let's see how we're going to make money on that meat."

They looked at me uneasily.

"How much does a serving of ribs weigh?" I asked.

Tyrus shrugged. "The customer gets half-a-pound with each serving."

"Good," I said, "that's the idea. Now how much do we get per serving?"

"Two and a quarter," Tyrus said quickly.

"So what's our gross per pound?" I asked optimistically.

They just looked at me.

"Sit down," I said to the boys. "What are you going to do when you get out of high school?"

Tyrus was fast. "Stay on with Road Buddy. I'll have one like it for myself one day."

I shook my head. "You won't have a damn thing until you learn about managing the business. Now listen, and listen carefully 'cause I'm not going to play games with you."

In the next two hours, I showed them how to figure gross weights, profits, overhead and how to increase or decrease profits by adjusting prices and cutting or adding help. They picked it up like a sponge picks up water.

By the time I was done, the boys were jubilant. "Wow," they said, "we didn't know there was so much to this!"

But part of me didn't share their jubilation. I was angry. These were smart, eager, young kids. All of them were seniors in high school, about to move into the community on their own. But school hadn't taught them the vaguest notion of how to compute percentages or other basic calculations. They weren't much ahead of Moose in their basic computational skills.

I was so damned mad that I slammed the office door and jumped in my car. I went to Forest High where the boys attended school and headed directly for the principal's office. I stood there impatiently, clenching and unclenching my fists while the secretary's fingers drummed on her typewriter. She glanced up once and returned to her typing.

"I want to see the principal," I said firmly.

A hint of surprise registered on her face. "Do you have an appointment?"

"No."

"Perhaps I can help you. Or one of the counselors." She was already cranking more paper into the machine.

I suddenly realized that I had come in my old work grubbies—dingy green coveralls with holes in the elbows and knees. My long underwear showed at the neck, sleeves, and ankles, and I hadn't shaved that morning. I began to wonder what impression the secretary had of me. Clearly, I didn't warrant any special treatment.

"I said I would please like to see the principal," I repeated slowly and precisely.

"Oh, Mr. Berger is in a meeting," she said, without looking up from her work.

The door to the principal's office was half-open, and I could see him at his desk. "Ma'am," I said in marked deference, "the principal seems to be back from his meeting now. Would you tell him that Chester Oden is waiting to confer with him?"

"I'll ask him if he'll see you now," she said.

Mr. Berger finally did see me. He brought me into his office and offered me a seat.

We exchanged pleasantries, including, as is the custom in Minnesota, a side discussion about the weather. Finally, he invited my problem.

I related my experience with the three black youths that morning, then asked, "How could these boys get to their senior year in high school without knowing how to compute percentages and ratios? Why don't they know what net weight is? Is this the case for most black students here?"

Berger sighed heavily and leaned back in his chair. He rustled with some papers on his desk as he gathered his thoughts. "Thirty percent of our enrollment is black. There was a time, a decade or so ago, when it was all white, when this was one of the better neighborhoods . . ."

"The good old days," I said wryly.

He glanced at me. In an instant we both knew where each was coming from. "Yes, times change," he sighed. He shook his head. "We have some trouble with white students . . ." he searched about the room for words. "But blacks! Less than two percent of them are in our upper track, and even the students with potential seem uninterested in helping themselves."

"What's the solution?" I said.

Berger shrugged.

"How many blacks on your football team?" I asked, changing my tack.

The principal closed his eyes, and his lips moved as he counted names. "Eight on the first string offense," he said. "Six on the second unit," he added and gave it more thought. "Seven on the defensive unit."

"Isn't it interesting that they perform above expectations on the athletic field?" I mused. "They seem able to perform up to their potential there, but not in the classroom."

Berger's response didn't surprise me. "That's typical," he said. "Our black students always do better at physical education than at academic subjects."

There was little doubt in my mind that a black kid coming to that school was influenced by the dominant philosophy that blacks are superior at athletics and inferior at learning. The kids were living up to the discriminatory expectations of other persons, especially educators.

As I went out of the office, a black parent was standing by the counter, waiting for the secretary to finish a letter. Finally she looked up.

"I'd like to see a counselor," the parent said. "Theo, that's my boy, was caught smoking under the grandstands again." There was a note of dejection and frustration in her voice.

I had come to Forest High angry. But when I left, I was both angry and depressed. I was in a funk about the school system's not taking black kids seriously. And my experience with the principal and his attitude toward blacks made me question once again the educational system's attitudes toward the mentally retarded. If black kids were not to be taken seriously, why should I think that kids like Moose would be taken seriously?

I decided to observe Moose's classes some more.

Moose had always loved school. For years he'd watched his older brother and sisters pick up their brown-bag lunches in the morning, toss their work pouches over their shoulders, and head out the door to school. And when Moose was old enough to go too, he was ready.

Polly had made Moose a big, bright cloth satchel with MOOSE emblazoned across the flap. She'd even sewn on a special pocket for potato chips. Moose carried everything to school in that satchel.

Moose loved school all right, but I believed there had to be more to learning than loving school. Moose's teachers had said they didn't want to push him. "He's making progress," they assured me, but I wondered.

In one class I observed, Moose's eyes danced whenever he successfully complied with the teacher's instructions.

"Take one block and put it on the table in front of you," the teacher said to the twelve children in Moose's class.

Moose obeyed gleefully.

"Now stack two blocks on the table." The teacher watched each child accomplish the task.

Impatiently, Moose nudged the boy next to him. His neighbor responded by poking his finger through Moose's small stack of blocks. Giggling, Moose leaned over to retrieve them from the floor.

"Do you need help, Moose?" the teacher asked.

"No hep!" Moose roared, dumping an oversized armload on the table.

"But you need only two blocks, Moose," the teacher explained patiently.

Moose folded his arms across his chest. I recognized his gesture. School was out for Moose for that day.

"Moose is a little stubborn," I told his teacher. "He likes to do things on his own and abandons them when something more interesting comes along."

"What is easy for one child can be difficult for another," she replied. "We're experimenting because we don't really know what Moose can learn. But we know one thing for sure. We don't want to frustrate the children by requiring that they perform skills beyond their capabilities."

The teachers at that school liked Moose, and Moose liked them, too, despite his occasional disobedience. Yet I was not aware of any significant progress. Apparently, a classroom for mentally retarded children was meant to be a happy place but not a learning place. This upset me, for I realized how important a decent education was for all kids. Without it, Tyrus and his friends would work for low wages a good part of their adult lives, and Moose would have to struggle along, dependent on whatever empathy he could receive from a world that considered him incapable of learning and accomplishing purposeful goals.

Soon after my talk with the principal, I plugged into a psychology program at the university, hoping that this would open a way for me to become involved with the issues that I cared about, the educational practices that affected Moose, blacks, and all of us. I confronted two more years of study and a very different career. My family life would change completely, too, but I didn't realize it then.

Chester Oden: married, father of a flock I hesitate to count, starting fresh in graduate school. Nuts? I wouldn't have argued with anyone who said I was!

After having been in research, it wasn't tough adjusting to the life of a grad student. It might have seemed grim, but things began to happen. Through a job running a small inner city project, I got into a conversation with a probation officer. We were talking about the difficulties blacks have in public schools. The probation officer was interested in the successes my own kids had experienced. He challenged me. "Would you take a ward of the state?"

I listened.

"Here is a boy who is very bright, but very screwed up. His social worker's folder on him is four inches thick. He thinks he's a tough hood and that he doesn't need anybody. But I think he's salvageable. Would you and your wife like to give him a try?"

I thought about it. We sure had the room in our old farmhouse, and here was a chance to try and help a black kid who was doing poorly in school. "How old is he?"

The probation officer smiled. He knew he had me hooked. "Eleven," he said.

Again I stopped to consider. I realized I'd be putting a lot of pressure on Polly, and I'd be asking the rest of the family to accept this kid as "one of our own." I went home to discuss the possibility with them.

The next day, I met with the probation officer. "Y'know," I said, "I'm in school, and away from home a lot. My oldest children are away from home, and my other children are still pretty young."

The probation officer was persuasive. "There are very few foster facilities for black kids in the community," he said. "This kid needs a place to stay badly. There aren't many options for him. He could go to St. Cloud, but you know that's like sending him to prison."

I offered to take B.J. home for a few nights, until the probation officer could find a more suitable placement for him.

"B.J.," I told him, "you're welcome here as long as you play it straight with us. No funny stuff, or I will personally throw your rear out into the snow and close the door behind you."

Two weeks later, the probation officer called and asked how B.J. was doing. Then he asked another favor. "There's Biddy," he began, "really a nice kid, but he doesn't have a family." Sure, we had room for Biddy.

Within a year, we had seven foster children. Now you can see why I consider it fortunate to have a large place.

Obviously, our kind of family situation takes some organization. We had a list of tasks that we laid out and posted on the ice-box, the one place where we could count on everybody looking at least several times a day. The tasks included cleaning the kitchen and garage, clearing the driveway, feeding and watering the horses, checking fences, and other chores. Each boy was assigned to a task for two weeks, so we knew immediately who was responsible for neglected tasks. We redesigned the basement along dormitory lines and built double bunks. We gave the boys bins for their clean clothes. We purchased dozens of white cotton socks and stencilled the sizes on them in india ink so that there would be minimal hassle extracting socks from the great laundry pile.

And, though you may not believe it, feeding seventeen isn't a whole lot different from feeding ten or so. Purchasing and preparing large amounts of food is an art but also a necessity in a large family. Then you have to quit worrying about whether or not this boy or that one has had enough to eat. We've found that when enough food is prepared to go around, no one really collapses of hunger. A hungry stomach is quite capable of finding leftovers.

While we had little trouble adapting to our family's

expanding size, the social organization required some adjustments. And, as you might suspect, Moose played an important part in that.

In early spring, Eric went to take his bike down off the storage rack and discovered that someone had beaten him to it. Half the spokes were broken out of the front tire. I told Eric to ask around; he'd discover what had happened. But something in the Oden household had changed—no one was owning up. I grilled Eric to make sure he hadn't broken it himself.

Then I decided to call all the boys together. All, that is, but Moose. Eric and the twins and Chris and David came in silently and parked their behinds. They looked down at the rug, because they knew what was coming. B.J. and Biddy joked in the doorway, and the others loitered nearby.

Finally, Eric turned his head. "Get in here, you guys, before Dad gets mad!"

I sat down, with the broken bike parts in front of me. "Okay," I said, "we have a broken bicycle, and it didn't break itself. What happened?" Silence. . . . "Alright, we're going to stay here until we all find out."

The first five minutes were a cacophony of denials, protestations that this home was full of shit, and accusations at me for being unfair and unreasonable.

"I haven't heard any facts about the bicycle," I said quietly, "but we have all night."

The boys looked at one another. Still no one spoke. They shifted uneasily.

Finally Steve, a diminutive kid, with a lot of tenacity looked around. "Why ain't Moose here?"

"Because Moose doesn't ride bicycles," I snapped. Then I thought, Maybe Moose *should* be here. "Moose!" I hollered. "Get your beautiful body in here!" Obviously eavesdropping, Moose popped his head around the corner.

"Moose," I said sternly. "Did you break Eric's bike?"

"Phooey!"

B.J. looked at Steve. "What are you calling out Moose for? You're the one who broke it."

Steve glared at B.J. "Not me! You got it down off the rack and dared me to ride it!"

"You was on the bike," Biddy said, "when you ran into the tractor!"

"You was on it, too!" Steve shouted, "and you, too, J.J., and you, Billie!"

"Naughty!" Moose said.

The room fell quiet. Five of the boys had been in on the accident. Four of them had been on the bike. At once.

"How are we going to fix the bike?" I asked.

The boys all looked at me. "I don't know how!" Steve pleaded.

"It'll cost fifteen bucks," I said, "if you don't know how. Who's going to pay for it?"

The boys all agreed to take a dollar a week out of their two-and-a-half dollar allowances for the next three weeks.

"Now, listen," I said. "There are rules in this house, and I'll lay them on you one more time. When you use someone else's things, you get permission. And you're responsible for returning them in the same shape you borrowed them. Got that?"

Everyone nodded.

"Then as far as I'm concerned, this incident is closed and forgotten. I don't want to hear another word about it. Dig?"

"Dig," they chorused.

So the skull session was born at our house.

I still didn't think it was important for Moose to attend the skull sessions, but that wasn't very bright of me, as I found out the next month.

The problem was B.J. He had bounced from one foster home to another. At first, we thought he remained sullen and failed to perform in school because of his bad experiences in white foster homes. But now he was into that pattern with us, and I really didn't know what to think. His teachers at school knew he was gifted but had long since given up on him ever living up to his potential. He had been placed in the lower track, and the entire school staff expected him to be passed on from grade to grade until he graduated out of everyone's hair. The periodic reports we got from school indicated that he was doing "borderline" work, and his reaction was a shrug.

But then the break came. We discovered that B.J. was stealing homework from the boys. A couple of the

teachers noticed a remarkable similarity between B.J.'s
work and that of several of our other boys, and they
called me in.

When I came home from talking with them I was
furious.

"Damn it, B.J., the thing that gets me is that you
have so much potential. Any of the boys in this house
would cut off their right arm to have your brains, and
you're happy to throw it away and let everyone think
you're a dummy."

He shrugged nonchalantly.

"And maybe you are a dummy," I snapped.

I decided to call a skull session and put B.J. on the
hot seat. When everyone had gathered, I laid out what I'd
learned from his teachers. Then I asked the group what
we ought to do about it. No one was thinking too kindly
of B.J. at this moment, for besides stealing homework,
he'd been teasing several of the boys, and he'd refused to
do his share of the chores.

The boys were normally very tolerant of each
other, but B.J. had stretched their tolerance to the
breaking point. One of the boys suggested that maybe
B.J. ought to spend a couple of weeks somewhere else,
while the rest of them cooled off enough to think about
the situation.

B.J. was quick to sense the tone of the meeting,
and he saw that his continued stay in the house might be
jeopardized. He looked around for an ally. "Hey,
Moose," he said, "what do you think of all this?"

Now nobody had ever really asked Moose his
opinion on problems or included him in any of the
decisions. Moose's eyes lit up at the opportunity. "You
naughty," he said to B.J.

"You're a turkey!" B.J. responded, trying to get
Moose to laugh.

"Phooey!" Moose said. "Naughty to steal! Naughty
to tease."

B.J. went over to Moose and tickled him. The rest
of us watched. "Aw come on, Moose. Who's your pal?"
B.J. said playfully.

Moose glared at him, then walked to the opposite
corner of the room and faced away.

His ploy for easy support foiled, B.J. fell silent. I
watched as B.J.'s smug expression gave way to

uncertainty. He seemed to reconsider. "Okay," he said finally, "I'll try to shape up."

Moose smiled broadly. That was about all Moose really needed from anybody. "B.J. my best friend," he said.

"Hey," said one of the other boys, "I thought you was my best friend."

"He's my best friend," another of the boys said.

Moose continued to grin. "B.J. my best friend," he said. Life was that simple for Moose, and the rest of the boys saw the beauty in that. Grudgingly, they agreed to give B.J. another chance. After all, it might be their turn to be on the hot seat next, and they wanted Moose to be heard then, too, so that they would get a fair shake. As I observed this, I realized how important Moose was to the little society we had.

Shortly after the B.J. incident, I experienced some of Moose's sense of fair play myself.

Report cards came out, and some of the boys had not done as well as I had insisted they do. There was a great deal of tension while they waited to see what I would do.

I called the boys together and sat down with them. I noticed that Moose was looking at me strangely. He seemed fascinated with the buttons on my sweater, staring at them from the time I sat down. I opened the meeting. "Okay, boys," I said, "let's have it."

"I sad, Daddy," Moose interrupted me.

"What do you mean?"

Moose got up, walked over to me, and pointed at my buttons. I looked down. The buttons had Thespian masks on them: a smiling mask and a frowning mask.

"He sad." Moose said, pointing to the frowning mask. "And I sad. Daddy naughty."

Finally it dawned on me. Moose was telling me that I had brought in my sweater with a lot of sad faces on it and that this was a lousy way to start a meeting. I could see what he meant. I took the sweater off and threw it outside the door.

Immediately Moose began to smile and the meeting got underway.

From that time on, Moose was an active participant in all our skull sessions. I'm not trying to say that Moose could figure out problems or suggest solutions better than anybody else. It was just that most of us were concerned with investigative matters, finding out who had done what and what should be done about it. Moose wasn't. Moose was concerned with how people felt and how they could be made to feel better. Caring isn't the only emotion that you need in a group of boys like I have, but it's an essential ingredient, and Moose was always there to provide it.

As much as I wanted to help Moose, as much as I cared about how he would cope with what he knew, I sometimes felt that he taught us a great deal more than we could teach him.

Polly and Aaron

Chet and Brett

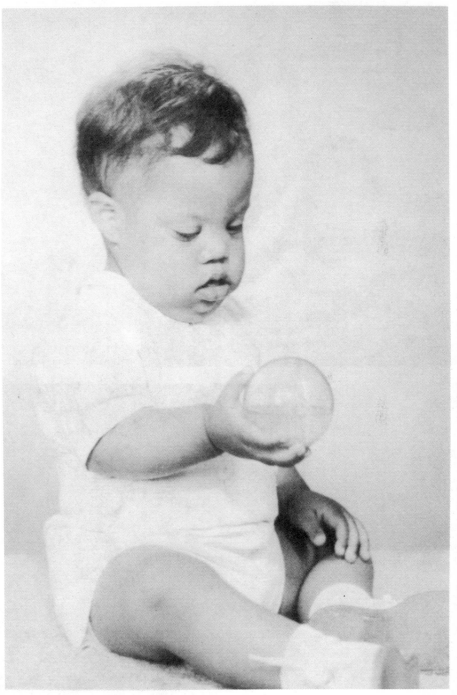

Moose, age eighteen months

Chris, age two,
and Moose, age seven

Moose, age ten

Moose, age ten

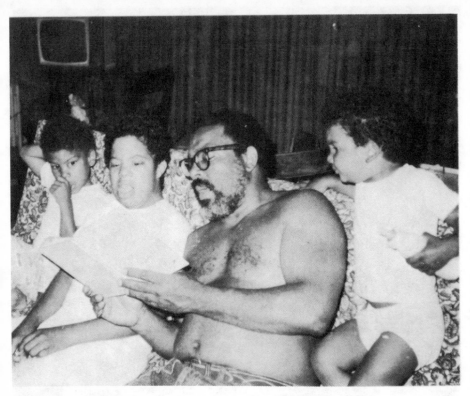

David, Moose, Chet, Brett

Moose, age thirteen

Moose, age fifteen

Moose, age thirteen

Grandma Pinkston and Moose

Moose and Mila

Moose, age fifteen

Moose, age eighteen

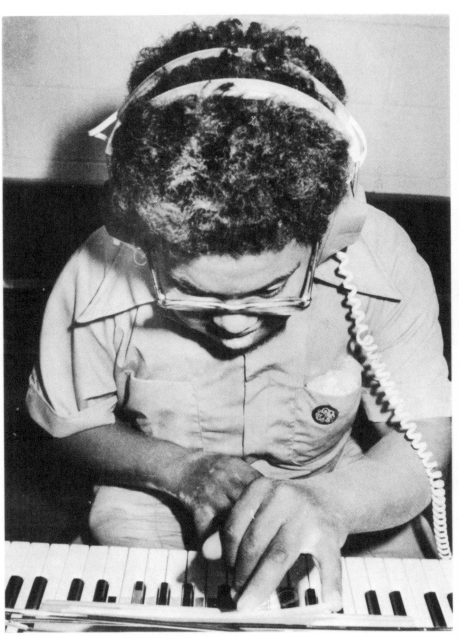

Moose, age eighteen

Front row: Aaron and Chris;
Second Row: Markel,
Brett, Mike, David, Eric

Chris, Eric, Michael, Markel

Front row: Markel, Lyndin, Steve, Ray, Wayne
Second row: Chris, Michael, Eric, Polly, Moose, Michael W., Chet
Third row: David, Aaron, Brett, Jeff

CHAPTER SEVEN

My last semester in graduate school was a bear. I worked full time in an inner city school, and took afternoon courses as well. It was the latter that involved us all in an incident we'll never forget.

After spending most of the day working with underachieving students, I'd come home and flop for a fast five minutes. The kids would pile into the van, Polly would toot the horn, and off we'd go. She'd drop me off at the University for my class, and they would head for the nearby park. The whole routine was relatively uncomplicated once we got into the swing of it. Relatively, that is, until John Wolfe entered the picture, adding a great deal of heat to an already torrid September.

John Wolfe looked like a teenager in spite of the fact that he was an associate professor of jurisprudence at the University of Minnesota. His reddish brown hair showered all over his head, no matter how he combed it. His eyes were clear hazel and freckles scattered across his face. John had a joyous smile, but it flitted away like a timid bird in uncertain situations. He spoke hesitantly, often haltingly, like his mind was racing ahead, discovering things on the tip of his tongue that shouldn't have been there.

To take the position at the University, John had moved his family to our neighborhood. Bridgette, his wife, and their two children, John Jr., ten, and Jimmy, eight, apparently came along only grudgingly.

Bridgette, however, soon became involved in community activities. So on the afternoons when she was away from home, John was without a car and the boys were without supervision. John wisely looked to the busiest people he could find for transportation and babysitting, and his attention was naturally drawn to us. Would we give him a ride to campus each afternoon? He'd get out with me and walk, so Polly would only have to make one stop. How could we refuse? Then he wondered if his boys could go with our boys to the park where Polly would keep an eye on them. I guess Polly's family calculation went something like this: a dozen plus two equals no additional trouble. So she agreed.

It soon became apparent that John Wolfe, in his delight at resolving both his babysitting and transportation problems, did not examine my family with sufficient scrutiny. I had told him that we were running a group home, and that probably created a particular impression, but at any rate, John climbed into the front seat of our van each afternoon with scarcely a glance toward the passenger compartment. What notice he did take of the Oden pups was not very discerning. I took all this for granted, because lots of parents had loaded their children in with ours with scarcely another thought.

But at the beginning of the third week, John came out of the house holding his two sons tightly by the hands. He came around to my window, smiled nervously, and commented on how nice and warm the day was.

"Yeah," I remarked dryly, "great for baking bread."

John cleared his throat. "Bridgette and I were talking . . ." He paused for me to say something, but I had the motor running and gave the gas pedal a light tap.

"Ah, is it true that you have a . . . well, that one of your boys . . ."

Honest to God, I still didn't know what he was driving at. "Hey, time's getting on," I said impatiently.

John still clung to his boys. "You have a son . . . isn't it Wayne . . . that's, ah . . ."

Polly snapped her head around and looked at him with a tinge of the old defensiveness. "Yes. He's retarded!"

John withered a bit under her stare. "I'm only, ah, concerned about the safety of, ah, Wayne, of course."

I looked at him closely. "Hey," I said, "if that's all

that's on your mind, get in. That's our problem, not yours."

John hesitated a bit longer. He looked into the back seat. Yes, it was crowded. "Is it . . . safe there? I mean, I know it is, I'm just asking."

Polly's eyes were blazing. "He's quite well supervised wherever he goes. And he enjoys playing in the park, just like the other boys."

John's eyes darted to his house. He tried to smile again, with difficulty. "I'm sure you can understand my concern," he said.

John and Jimmy stood there, clinging to their father's hands, their hair neatly combed. They were wearing bright, new blue jeans and shirts, and their shoes were scuffless.

"Yes, maybe I can understand," I said. "But can you understand that I don't want to be late for class?"

John Wolfe took his kids around to the back and let them in. They scrambled into two small places that were made for them and sat stiffly against the sides of the van. These were the same boys who had been playing and laughing with the Oden gang last week without any sign of tension. Now, as they got into the van, they appeared to fear for their lives. I could only shake my head and wonder about the judgment of parents and the influence that adults have over impressionable children. But I had plenty of consolation in this case. I knew that ten minutes after John was out of their sight, they'd forget whatever bullshit he and Bridgette had loaded on them and go back to interacting with our boys as if nothing had happened. The bullshit might get to them in a few years, but the boys were still at the age when a touchdown pass was still a touchdown pass, regardless of who threw it.

John came around and got into the car. "Sure," he said suddenly, "let's go. Nothing to worry about." We drove in silence for several miles while John continued to stare into space, apparently still trying to resolve what was weighing rather heavily on his mind.

When we got to campus, John got out of the car and started out in the wrong direction. He stopped short in his tracks, reddened with embarrassment, and waved. "Thanks for the ride," he mumbled, and took off without saying anything to John Jr. or Jimmy.

John's concerns had irked Polly. I could understand her feelings, because John appeared to her to be responding to the label, "Down's syndrome," or whatever label he had suddenly tacked onto Moose. And that always bugs Polly, especially in a person like John who was obviously educated. Isn't part of education separating reality from stereotypes? John was, in Polly's eyes, acting like a person who was afraid of a ghost. He had heard something frightening about Moose, and instead of checking to see whether or not there was a real basis for his anxiety, he feared Moose. He'd been in the same car with Moose several times. His boys had played with Moose the previous week, and now, all of a sudden, he was responding to a label and disregarding his own experience. Polly was very sensitive about people who responded to Moose as if he were a label, rather than the person she had come to know him to be.

Over the next few days, Polly and I were rather uncomfortable with John. However, he had an opportunity to relieve at least some of his fears, firsthand. We picked him up after classes one warm Friday evening, and he said he wanted to drop by a market on the way home to get some fixings for supper. We suggested a stop at the park and a beer with us first.

When we got to the park, we turned the kids loose and sat down under an oak tree, thankful for the plentiful shade it provided.

I observed John's keen surveillance of the children. This was the first time he had stopped to watch his children at play with ours, and I wondered what he was thinking. The kids were playing tag, but it could have been baseball, or chase, or kick-the-can, and the results would have been the same. Anybody but little Brett, who still didn't motor well, could catch Moose in a foot race, so he was "it" most of the time.

This seemed to bother John. As he watched the kids, he clucked his tongue, disapprovingly. "Isn't that too bad?" he said tentatively, looking for our reactions. When neither of us reacted to his comment, he sat up and observed the children more closely. On went the game just as before. The kids began racing backwards on their hands and knees, and of course, Moose came in last, giving every other child the chance to be winner. Finally, the scene got to John. He turned to me and asked, "Why? Why?"

I looked at him, "Why what?"

John voiced several thoughts that had apparently been going through his head. "Why isn't he with other retarded children? Isn't this treatment cruel? Wouldn't he better off if. . . ."

Polly stiffened, ready to dive in on John like a mother panther whose cubs were in danger.

"Wait a minute," I said to John. "I'd like you to observe Moose a little more closely while I point out something to you." John fixed his eyes on the kids, who were centering a lot of their activity about Moose, the defined "loser" in the group. "Have you ever been to an institution?" I asked John. "If you have, then you know that Moose would not get this much attention in an entire month. Look out there. Somebody's got to be a loser, and everyone knows it will be Moose. Including Moose. But notice that the kids aren't hurting him. They're playing *with* him, and he's loving it. Have you seen him do anything but smile and enjoy himself? Being included in the group is a helluva lot better from his standpoint than sitting in a roomful of kids who wouldn't react to him at all. It's much better than having to occupy himself with the same playthings day after day with only the occasional attention of a social worker or psychologist. Think about it."

The kids formed a line while we were chatting and picked sides for kickball. Moose, the last to be chosen, stood on the sidelines, his mouth hanging open as he looked sadly on.

"Look," John said. "Just look at that. He's going to be left out. Is that what you call a lot of fun?"

I watched the kids and didn't answer. They began to form sides and lay out the bases while Moose remained a solitary figure on the sideline. Then Eric saw Moose and waved his hands, shouting, "Hold on, gang. Come on, Moose. Join us." Moose turned on the sun within him. He tippy-toed over to Eric, his arms flailing. The other kids may not have been elated at this addition to their team, but even so, they all cheered and clapped him on board.

"Interesting thing about kids," I said, "you really have to teach them about manners and those sorts of things. No child I know was born saying 'please' and 'thank you.' And they have to learn to take turns. But that," I said, pointing to the field, "is something I never had to teach my children. This time Eric included Moose. Next time it's likely to be Mike, and the next time Markel will pitch in. That's the way it works. I don't really want Moose to have to grow up knowing only retarded kids. That wouldn't be much of a life for him."

"Noble thoughts," John said skeptically, "noble thoughts."

As the days went by, John Wolfe became more comfortable with our arrangement. He seemed to relax, and he chatted with the boys several times as we rode along. He even tried to talk to Moose; but Moose didn't pay much attention to him, and John was easily dissuaded from that communication.

There were some changes in his sons, too. John, Jr. and Jimmy were taking more interest in sports and weren't so upset by dirty pants and shirts. John seemed to approve.

One day he said seriously, "I do appreciate the rides, Chet. I know it must not look like it, but I do appreciate them. Is there something I can do for you in return?"

I laughed. When a person has to ask, I always take him only half-seriously. "Put truck springs in the van; make easier riding for everyone," I joked.

One day in October, we hit the park with our six-pack of aren't-we-glad-it's-Friday-afternoon celebration, stopped the van, and popped the tops on a couple of brews.

It was still warm, so the children took off their shoes. Then they invented a game in which they made footprints in the sand. Periodically they would stop, and the child who was "it" had to figure out who had done what by "reading" the footprints.

While this was going on, Moose was very busy with something else, his activities partially obscured by the sides of the sand pile. After awhile, we tooted the horn and the kids came running. Polly leaned out the window and called, "Your shoes, don't forget your shoes."

The kids screeched to a halt; then reversed their steps to go back after their shoes. Moose came tottering toward the car, stirring up a small dust storm with his tiny steps. I noticed a silly grin on his face but didn't think any further of it. Soon, however, I discovered that Moose's expression was a clue to his activities during the game. "Hey!" Eric shouted in a war whoop, "someone's stolen my shoes."

"Mine, too!" Jimmy exclaimed, and echoes followed from all the other kids.

Moose giggled.

"Okay, Moose," I said, catching on. "Where are the shoes?"

Moose gave me some of his double talk.

"Moose," I said, "I know that isn't talk and you know it isn't talk. I asked you, 'Where are their shoes?'"

Moose broke up laughing, laid down on his back, rolled over on his side, and slapped his knees gleefully.

"Come on, Moose. Let's get with the shoes, or I'll leave you here while the rest of us go home to eat."

Moose continued to roar with laughter.

John Wolfe chimed in, "What the hell's going on?"

Finally, Polly ran out of patience. "Wayne Oden! Where are your shoes?"

"Not Wayne; Moose."

"Wayne Oden, find the shoes."

Slowly, still enjoying his prank, Moose walked toward a tree near the sandbox. There, in the branches, were the shoes Moose had carefully hidden.

John turned to me. "Did you see that? I mean, did you see that?" John watched Moose for a long moment, mulling the incident over in his head. "That's great," he said, finally. "That's really great." John sounded at ease for the first time since I'd met him.

The fall turned chilly, but the events that followed would be warming things up again very soon. At least for the Wolfes and the Odens.

One afternoon our boys and John's boys began playing "workup" in the park with another group of kids. In workup, the batter is against the rest of the players. Each time a batter makes an out, he goes to right field and works himself up through the rest of the positions until he becomes batter again.

Jimmy Wolfe patiently worked his way up to the batter's box. There, he began bragging to Ashley, a boy who had sprained his ankle and was acting as "ump."

"I'm gonna knock the ball out of the park," Jimmy crowed.

The pitcher delivered the ball. Jimmy swung and missed by two feet.

"Strike one," called Ashley.

The pitcher arched another ball toward Jimmy.

"Strike two."

Jimmy stepped in front of the plate. "Hey, you creep," he shouted to the pitcher, "stop burning them in."

"I'm rainbowing them," the pitcher denied angrily. He took the ball and tossed another pitch. Jimmy swung at a ball that was over his head.

"Strike three," Ashley shouted.

"Drat!" Jimmy slammed the bat to the ground. He'd worked long and hard to get his "ups." He turned to Ashley. "Gimme another swing."

"You had your three," Ashley responded.

Jimmy looked out to right field. It was a long way out there. "Gimme another swing," he insisted, "or I'll knock your block off."

"That's cheating." Ashley accused. "Whaddya wanta spoil our game for?"

By this time the boys closest to the plate, including John Jr., were getting mad at Jimmy, too, for not taking up his position in right field. A couple of them moved toward him. But Jimmy didn't notice.

"Who're you calling a cheater?" he screamed at Ashley. Jimmy dove for Ashley, taking him down.

"Lemme go," Ashley hollered. "You're hurting my ankle."

"Say 'Uncle,'" demanded Jimmy.

They scuffled some more, but Jimmy had the upper hand.

"Uncle," said Ashley finally, fighting back tears.

"I guess I showed you," said Jimmy as Ashley clambered to his feet.

Polly, John Wolfe, and I had seen the scuffle and were about to intervene, when it stopped just as abruptly as it began. We figured we'd let the kids work out the problem themselves and went back to our conversation.

In a matter of moments, we heard shouts again and looked up to see a crowd of boys gathered in a circle. The shouting grew louder.

"Give it to him, Moose!"

"Choke him!"

"Way to go, Moose!"

My head began to spin. Moose? What was happening with Moose? I couldn't see because the knot of boys obscured my vision, but I had that familiar feeling in my stomach that comes with trouble. I jumped to my feet and raced for the group.

Six boys—I'll never forget it; the picture is engraved in my mind—surrounded Moose and Jimmy Wolfe. They were shouting for Moose to choke Jimmy. John Wolfe hollered, "My God!" from somewhere behind me. Moose was clutching Jimmy around the neck with both hands. Jimmy's face was purple and his body quivered as if the last bit of life had been shaken out of him. The boys were shrieking at the top of their lungs.

"Way to go, Moose!"

"Kill him."

At my appearance, the boys ran in all directions. "Moose!" I bellowed. Moose looked at me and dropped Jimmy at once. He stood there, frozen, as if he suddenly realized he was doing something wrong. Jimmy was not breathing. I opened his mouth, extracted his tongue, and began to give him mouth-to-mouth resuscitation. In the background I could hear a great commotion as people gathered around to see what was going on.

Moose tugged at my sleeve. "Daddy, Daddy. I not mad. Ashey's game. I pay Ashey's game."

I heard David ask Polly, "Momma, why is Daddy kissing Jimmy?"

"Oh no!" was all I heard John say.

"Is he all right?" Polly shouted. "Is he all right?"

I continued mouth-to-mouth resuscitation.

Then John seemed to come to his senses. "Damn it! I told you, you couldn't trust that kid. I just knew you couldn't trust him!"

Jimmy finally regained breathing. An ambulance wheeled up with a scream and a flash. The attendants waved me away and Jimmy disappeared on a stretcher, his dad close behind. The siren cut the air and the ambulance took off. As if its exit were a signal that the accident was over, the bystanders began to drift away, still unclear about what had happened. I could hear the beginnings of rumors involving Moose and Jimmy. But at this point, I really didn't care who thought what.

I went to Moose, who was terrified after seeing my rage, and I put my arm around him. "What happened?" I asked, as calmly as I could. I'd never seen Moose hurt anyone before.

Moose babbled in his incomprehensible way, and kept saying, "Ashey's game. Boys pay." Eric was at my heels, and we tried to piece together what had happened.

"Ashley Myers and some of the other guys were mad at Jimmy so they sicked Moose on him," Eric said. "They told Moose it was a game." The pieces of the puzzle fell into place.

"My God," I said. "My God."

Moose was looking at me, his eyes large and inquisitive. "Naughty, naughty," he said, shaking his head solemnly.

"You're very strong, Moose," I said. "You mustn't use your strength against people. Those other boys were wrong. They should not have told you to squeeze Jimmy's neck."

"Naughty, naughty to pay," Moose said to himself, slapping his own wrist.

"We will go see Jimmy and tell him you love him."

Moose brightened up a little. "I say sorry."

"Yeah, Moose, right," I said.

Polly and I headed for the hospital. Jimmy was in an intensive care unit. A nurse said the doctor was with him and that Jimmy was in shock.

John Wolfe was there, shaking his head and wringing his hands. He seemed to be struggling to believe what had happened to his son. I went over to John and put a heavy hand on his shoulder. I opened my mouth, but not much came out. "I'm terribly sorry for what happened. . . ."

Without taking his eyes off the floor, John said evenly, "This all seems like a bad dream. I should have known this would happen. Bridgette will never forgive me. I should have known this was going to happen."

There was a long silence. "Does Bridgette know?" I asked.

John sank deeper into himself. "Yeah. She's on her way over now."

"If you don't mind I'd like to stay," I said.

John remained silent. We all hung around, alternately sitting and pacing. Waiting.

Just then a woman I knew to be Bridgette burst down the hall. A nurse was at her elbow, talking rapidly, but futilely. Bridgette barely spoke to John and went into the room where Jimmy was. She remained in the room only a few minutes, and then she came out amid a volley of short, piercing exchanges with the doctors. She began to sob softly and looked at Jimmy's door, as if her mental efforts would assist in the recovery of her son. Polly went up to Bridgette and put her arm around her. I approached her too, but stopped a few feet away. "If there is anything I can do . . ." I began, but then I realized she probably didn't know who I was.

She looked at Polly and me questioningly and shook us off as if we were old garments. "Who the hell are they?" she said to John.

John leaned toward her. "They're the parents of the boy who . . ."

The look she gave Polly and me can only be described as hateful. There were tears of rage in her eyes as she glared at us. Her breathing became choppy and deeper as she mustered her forces. "You're criminals," she accused loudly, "the worst kind of negligent criminals. Letting that . . . that freak loose on a playground full of children."

Nearby, the medical staff fell silent.

"We're sorry it happened," was all I could think of to say.

"I warned John. I know what kind of a boy your son is."

"You're upset," Polly said. "And you have reason to be. I hope to God your son is all right. I'll pray for him."

"I think it would be better to talk with you about this a little later," I said to Bridgette.

"I hope I never see you again," she answered.

There wasn't a lot more to say, so we left.

At mid-morning the next day, we called the hospital and asked about Jimmy Wolfe. They wouldn't tell us anything about his condition because we were not immediate family. We called the Wolfes and asked if we could come over. Neither Polly nor I talked about it explicitly, but I guess we both anticipated that after a good night's sleep, Bridgette would have recovered her composure.

When we arrived at the Wolfes', John opened the door and stepped out on the front porch. He wouldn't look directly at us, and he seemed terribly uncomfortable. "Jimmy's okay," he said at last, "but they're keeping him under observation." He glanced inside and shook his head. "I don't know what will happen . . ." he rambled on, "I shouldn't say anything."

"Hey," I said, "is Bridgette still that upset?"

He looked me squarely in the eye for just an instant. "I should have known this would happen." His expression was pleading, as if he wanted me to agree with him.

"John," I said, "there was no way of knowing. Moose has never hurt a fly. Some bad things happened . . ."

Suddenly Bridgette stepped outside and pulled the door almost shut behind her.

Obviously we were not welcome.

"I want you to know I called my lawyer," she said tightly.

"Your lawyer?" I stepped back. "Your lawyer?" I guess I should have suspected that, from the way she had reacted the previous night. I should have added it all up to this total. But I was dumbfounded. "What did you tell your lawyer?"

"In the first place," Bridgette said, "I want *him* institutionalized immediately. Then I am preferring criminal charges against you as his parents."

I looked at her steadily. I guess I knew how she felt, and I grieved for her. "My son, Moose, is big for his age, and he's very strong," I tried to explain as softly and as clearly as I could. "But he is a gentle person who has never done a hostile thing in his life. He is also very gullible."

Bridgette's body tensed until the cords stuck out in her neck. Her fists clenched at her sides. "He's a maniac and a potential murderer. How can you be so calm when you have a monster going free in your household?"

"Please understand," I said, "I am deeply grieved that this happened to Jimmy. But I would also like you to know how it happened. A group of boys, apparently Jimmy's own friends, goaded Moose into doing it. Moose did not know he was hurting Jimmy." I looked at John and John looked at me. He had seen the incident develop, and I could see him reviewing it in his mind. He seemed to grow visibly smaller, afraid to open his mouth.

"I want you to leave our property now!" Bridgette demanded.

"Just a minute, please, honey," John said. "Let's hear Chet out." He extended his hand to her as a sign of support, but she brushed it away.

"I was there, honey," he said in a last attempt to gain her attention.

"And you let our son be strangled by a mindless monster!"

John shot a quick glance in my direction and then looked down.

Bridgette took him by the shoulder. "Order these . . . people off our property immediately!"

Polly turned to go, and I half turned to follow suit. "You really don't need to," I said quietly, "we didn't come to fight. We just wanted you to know how sorry we are."

* * *

We went to the bimonthly PTA meeting a few weeks later because we heard that the subject of Jimmy Wolfe and Moose might be raised. We knew Jimmy had been taken off the critical list, and we were relieved. But we also knew that the incident was not over.

Polly and I were seated in the center of the room. From my left, I heard one woman ask, "How's your son, Mrs. Wolfe?" I didn't catch Bridgette's answer, for just then the chairman called the meeting to order. Ignoring the gavel, Bridgette rose, and without waiting for the chair's recognition, turned to face the group. "Many of you are aware that my son Jimmy has only recently recovered from a brutal attack," she began, stridently. "It is Jimmy's attacker I wish to discuss." A murmur broke out among the parents seated around us.

John Wolfe stood for an instant. "Can we just get on with the meeting?" His voice was weak.

Bridgette ignored John's half-hearted attempt to head her off. She glared at her husband, then paused for a long moment.

A voice called out, "What are you going to do?"

"I'm going to take John Jr. and Jimmy out of public school," she answered emphatically. "And they will not go to the public playgrounds or parks until the school board or the courts do something about the menace living in our community." A stir began around Bridgette and spread throughout the audience. "The board must take action to expel Wayne Oden from our school system. He threatens all of our children."

There was silence as parents tried to digest what she had said and to seek some basis on which to form an opinion.

"I have one son who has been savagely attacked. God spared him. I won't risk his safety or my other son's safety any more.

"There are some parents who don't care what their children do," she continued. "Well, we can't stand for that—we've got to demand action."

A scattering of applause indicated that Bridgette had some support for her view.

I had sensed this nightmare would happen when we met at the Wolfes' house. And I understood why Bridgette felt so strongly—but I wasn't going to sit by and let my child get run over. I stood and raised my hand. "I am Chet Oden, the father of the child who unfortunately hurt Jimmy Wolfe. I am deeply sorry about that. I say that here, publicly, as I have already said it privately to Mr. and Mrs. Wolfe.

"But now we have another matter. What is to be done with Moose? Must he be institutionalized to make this school, this town, safe for other children? Moose, in all of his twelve years, has hurt another person in our family only once; that was when we brought Eric home from the maternity ward, and Moose hugged him too tightly. We showed Moose how to love a baby, and he has not hurt our babies since. And we have had a lot of babies in our family."

I heard a scattering of nervous laughter.

"Moose is not hostile, and he does not strike others in anger." I looked about the room. Parents seemed to be listening to me. "I have taught my children to settle their differences verbally, not with their fists. No parent here has a child who has been attacked by an Oden.

"Moose was carefully instructed, cajoled, ordered by at least six children to grab Jimmy Wolfe and play a game called 'choke Jimmy.'" I paused and looked around.

"Moose did not know he was hurting Jimmy. He has not yet learned his own strength. Yes, Moose did it. He was like a loaded pistol picked up by six boys. I saw them, but I can't put names to their faces. I think some of you can. If we want to get at the truth, we'll have to do it together."

Confusion and low talking.

"Don't make excuses for your son!" Bridgette interrupted. "He nearly killed my boy, and he should pay the consequences."

Again, John Wolfe stood. "Wait a minute," he began, but I couldn't make out John's words above the noise of the crowd. Quickly, Bridgette pulled him down into his seat.

A tall, well-groomed man jackknifed out of the crowd and silenced much of the buzzing. "I'm Gerry Meyers," he said. "While I'm not involved, I do have a question. I appreciate your point that some other kids taunted your son, Dr. Oden, but isn't he responsible for his own actions?"

I nodded toward Meyers. "In answer to your question, Mr. Meyers, my son, Moose, is a Down's syndrome child. In some ways he has limited mental abilities. But I consider him a responsible boy. Moose doesn't have the capacity to purposefully harm anyone. But sometimes his actions are not what he thinks they are. He cooperated with the rest of the boys there because he trusted their judgment. Moose, more than the rest of us in this room, *must* trust others. Moose trusted his peers and complied with their commands too closely. Are you telling me I must start teaching Moose to distrust people?"

Then from somewhere in the darkness of my memory, a name emerged. I struggled to retrieve it, but it eluded me. "Ashey," I said half aloud. "Ashey." Then it hit me. Eric had said the name, Ashley Meyers. "By the way, Mr. Meyers," I asked, "do you have a son named Ashley?"

Before he had a chance to reply, Bridgette leaped to her feet. "I'm going to take you to court! I want your boy to answer for his attack on my son."

"Actually, it might help if a court of law were to examine the situation," I interjected. "It might help us discover what really happened."

As I said this, I watched John Wolfe. He was edgy, looking for a way to escape. I waited for him to stand up and be counted. Apparently, he would require a lot of nudging.

"Wait just a moment," I called out. "There is a person here who saw the incident with me. I think he has something to say." My eyes were on John. Suddenly there was silence as everyone focused on him. He looked at me, furtively at first, but our eyes locked, and he knew I was talking to him.

He stood tentatively, then straightened himself up. Bridgette's hands pulled at his coat, and he shook them off. She grasped him more firmly and tried to force him back into his seat, but he looked at her calmly. "Please, dear, I have something to say," he said. "I'm John Wolfe," he introduced himself in a clear, steady voice. "I guess I'm as upset by all this as anyone. We all have children, and they seem so terribly, terribly fragile." He sighed. "And it's difficult for fathers . . . and mothers, too, to know what is best for them." His face was gentle as he looked directly at Bridgette.

John paused. Then went on, "I know Moose. I know he is a Down's syndrome child. And I was warned that he might be dangerous." John looked down for a moment. "Y'know, I don't believe Moose is dangerous . . . and I feel no animosity toward him." He turned to the crowd. "I hope there is no trial. I really don't feel Jimmy needs it. Or anyone else."

Meyers stood again. "Wouldn't it help to find out who is responsible and who isn't?"

John Wolfe grimaced. "Well. . . . see, Chet has a point. . . ."

"Moose attacked Jimmy!" Bridgette interrupted.

John shook his head. "Actually, Bridgette, you didn't see what happened. I did. And it's just not that simple."

For the first time, Bridgette's expression changed. "My God, John," she said fearfully. "Is there something you haven't told me?"

John looked at her for a long minute. "Not really." Then he turned to Meyers. "I really don't know what a court would find," he said. "And if Chet filed against the six boys, or caused the state to file against them. . . ." Suddenly he unburdened himself. "I think our own John Jr. was one of the six, and I think Ashley Meyers was also one."

John suddenly looked as if a great weight had been lifted from his shoulders. "Chet," he said seriously, "you and your family have been very tolerant of the Wolfes. I want to publicly thank you. It appears as though some of us have homework to do with our own children."

The meeting broke up shortly after that.

After Polly and I got into the van, she turned to me and asked, "Suppose John Jr. hadn't been involved. Do you think Bridgette would have taken this to court? Do you think John Wolfe would have let her?"

I shrugged. "I don't know," I said, "there are a lot of people who believe the things she was saying in there."

"God," Polly sighed, "what would have happened to Moose?"

I didn't answer. I think she knew as well as I.

When we got back to the house, Moose was waiting for us at the front door. He knew we'd seen Jimmy's parents. "Jimmy okay now?"

I hugged Moose and kissed him on the cheek. "Moose, you're a good boy. I think we'll see Jimmy and John Jr. at the park pretty soon."

Moose stuck his thumb in his mouth and smiled around it.

CHAPTER EIGHT

By the time Moose was sixteen, Polly and I were still unable to accurately assess his potential for learning.

At home, he would learn about things he liked or was interested in. But when it came to even simple language arts or number skills, he would only laugh us off.

We had hoped the schools would help Moose where we'd been unsuccessful. But they didn't give us much satisfaction.

"We can't really set standards," Moose's teachers continued to tell us. "We can only teach these children as much as they're willing to learn."

I guess Polly and I came to accept that. But then Fosse Johnson came along and proved us all wrong. He turned our heads around, forcing us to consider that Moose might have more learning ability than anyone gave him credit for.

I never really heard the whole story of why Fosse Johnson was sent to us, and I didn't ask. I don't want to know what a guy has done wrong; I want to know what he wants to do that's right and how he plans on achieving it. I only knew that Fosse had been in several foster homes and could make himself about as popular as a swarm of mosquitoes under the netting.

Fosse arrived at our house early one summer morning when all of the boys except Chris were still in bed. When school is out, the boys tend to stay up later at night, and TNT can't get them up in the morning. But just the sound of the doorbell when Fosse rang it was different. I brought him inside the house into the mud room where everyone is expected to take off their shoes, and I knew right away we'd all remember Fosse Johnson. He was just over five feet tall, and he wasn't just thin. He was emaciated. His arm was about the size of my thumb, and I towered over this little shaver like the Jolly Green Giant.

I motioned for him to bring in his duffle bag, which was still on the doorstep. He smiled easily and shrugged. The bag was as big as he was, and he didn't even try to budge it. So here was our city slicker, a few hours away from starvation and too frail to pick up his own underwear.

Chris, four years younger than Fosse, yanked up the bag with one hand and trailed off into the dorm where Fosse would be quartered, muttering all the way about how Fosse was going to have real problems when he started feeding the horses.

Like a mouse inspecting a new cage, Fosse quickly poked his head into the other boys' rooms and looked about him. Apparently satisfied with what he found, he relaxed. His arm shot out. "I'm Foster Johnson," he said to me, "but if you want to get along with me, call me Fosse."

I suppressed my amusement. "I'm Chet Oden. Call me Uncle Chet. Or Mr. Oden. Or even Dr. Oden. Call me whatever you like. Just follow our rules and you'll make it here real fine."

"Lay the rules on me, Dr. Oden," Fosse said boldly, "and we'll negotiate them."

We had been talking quietly, but the vibes must have been heavy. All the boys were unaccountably up now, and they began to gather around us. Some of them were still rubbing sleep out of their eyes, but even in their sleepy condition, they observed intently this skinny little kid who stood his ground with me.

Fosse reacted to the gathering crowd by broadening his casual smirk. I anticipated that the sea of black faces might intimidate him, but if they did, he didn't show it a bit. His brashness was like a line between us that he challenged me to step across.

"These rules don't bend," I said quietly. "Keep your hands to yourself. That means no stealing and no fighting for *any* reason. I expect you to go to school regularly and to improve your grades steadily. I expect you to get into some self-improvement, whether it's ballet, or playing the violin, or learning to speak German. And I expect you to do your chores. When I ask a question, I expect the truth. Do you understand what I've said?"

Fosse continued to grin at me. "Hey, man, what a swinging pad. Who designed this place? It's like, out of Star Trek."

"Look, Fosse, I just laid some rules on you. Now two things will get you back to court services fast: one, breaking any of the rules; two, having the rest of the boys vote you out. They're a tolerant bunch, but only up to a point."

Fosse pursed his lips. "Hey, man," he said, suddenly accommodating, "I hear you. I'm gonna get into your heads. Don't worry yourself on my behalf."

I sighed. "The sweat period is three weeks. You dig?"

Fosse took out a cigarette and paused before he touched the fire to the end. "Mind if I smoke?" he said.

I didn't crack a smile. "Not at all. On the way to the slam."

Fosse got the message. He snapped out the light and handed me the pack. "Guess I won't be needing these."

The boys broke their silence, chuckling at Fosse's apparent fall.

But Fosse was fast and Fosse was smooth. I felt the rest of the boys' eyes on my back as they watched this kid spar with me. "No sweat, guys," he said to them. "Really. I just got put in my place. I can dig that." For Fosse, our dialog was like playing the piano. Begin two words of any sentence, and he could pick out the rest of the tune by ear. The kids stood back a little, awed by his impromptu.

"Some barn," Fosse said, again changing his tack. "You've gotta be some heavy dude to put the key in *this* door."

"Fosse," I said quietly, "you can jive me all you want. You can go a long way in the adult world with bullshit. But I'm going to say this one time so you know where I'm coming from. Action. Don't bluff; I'll call. Don't fake me; I remember and so do the boys. You're here to improve your school work and your personal habits. You can wag your tongue as long as you're cutting a trail.''

I introduced Fosse to the boys, impressed by his quick wit and ability to say something to each of them in a way to gain their positive reaction. He turned each one on as easily as a light switch. Fosse Johnson was a real con artist.

Finally, I introduced Fosse to Moose. Moose was about the same age as Fosse, but about six inches taller and nearly twice Fosse's weight. Fosse looked at Moose, did a double take, and then gaped, as if he had seen someone from Mars. Moose blinked back at Fosse stoically, waiting for Fosse to make the first move.

Fosse took half a step toward Moose but stopped short. Moose had his usual cold and was having trouble breathing through his nose. Some spittle ran down the corner of his mouth. He was getting a little nervous and began sucking his thumb.

For a moment, Fosse was speechless. He searched from one boy to another and picked out Biddy with uncanny judgment. At over six feet and two hundred pounds, Biddy was physically the most powerful of the boys. Biddy was an open, rather simple, and very affable youth. ''Hey, man, I like your Kojak,'' Fosse grinned, referring to Biddy's cleanly shaven head. ''What's the low-down on this guy?'' Fosse jerked a thumb toward Moose.

Biddy smiled at the flattery and started to say something, but the tight expressions of the other boys stopped him cold. He hung onto his words, and the smile died on his face.

Fosse looked from face to face and for the first time encountered an unfriendly challenge. He turned to me. ''Dr. Oden,'' he said smoothly, ''let's have it. What's with Moose? I mean, does he talk? Or does he lurk in the shadows and then leap out at people?''

Fosse's grin suggested he was anticipating a hearty laugh at Moose's expense.

Silence.

''I mean, the guy just ain't quite right,'' Fosse persisted.

I ignored his reference to Moose. When a guy digs himself into a hole, it's up to him to dig himself out. ''The sweat period is three weeks,'' I repeated. ''After that time, we all get together again to decide if we want you to stay. And during that time you can decide whether or not you like us. We don't want any boys here who don't really want to be here. If we agree that you will be staying, we'll make a three-month pact: You must agree to make some real gains, and we'll agree to back you all the way in your efforts. It's a two-way street."

Fosse gave me a sidelong glance. Quickly, he assessed the situation. Then, like an actor rehearsing in front of a mirror, Fosse turned on a smile. Resigned, he slapped his sides to generate some momentum and approached Moose, hand outstretched. "Hi, ol' buddy," he said cheerily, "I'm Fosse Johnson."

Moose had been standing there for a full fifteen minutes, talked about as if he were carved from wood. But his ears weren't pine, and his feelings weren't petrified. Moose spun around on his heel. "Phooey!" he spat.

You got it, Moose, I thought, you got it.

The boys leaped at the chance to express their feelings. "Hey, boy," they chided Fosse, "you got left waving in the breeze."

Fosse paused; then came that easy grin. "That's another one on me," he admitted. "I mean, fellas," he said, in an exaggerated appeal to the group, "if you want to kick me out right here and now, just say the word. I can take it." Fosse had the boys pegged right. They weren't about to vote him out until he'd had a fair chance. He realized he'd made a mistake picking on Moose, but the boys weren't mad enough to deprive Fosse of an opportunity to prove himself. And Fosse knew it.

I continued to be amazed at this newcomer. He was street-wise, but more than that, he had already learned how to handle the other boys. Fosse was definitely going to make his presence known and felt.

"Hey," I said, "I don't know about the others, but I'm not tired of your face. Yet. You can run your mouth all you want around here. Just remember: school grades, chores, and rules."

Fosse looked down. "I'll get into his head," he said, nodding in Moose's direction, "and yours. No sweat, man."

"I hope you get into yours while you're at it," I added.

The first week, I made the mistake of asking Fosse which chores he would prefer. He said he wanted to feed and corral the horses. He claimed he wanted fresh air and a chance to see real, live animals. Actually, I suspected that he didn't give a hang for the horses but wanted an excuse to get out of the house and tap a fag, but I didn't let on. There would be plenty of time to work it out if my suspicions were correct, and I certainly didn't want to put any ideas in his head if I was wrong.

From the start, Fosse displayed a trait which was to become even more obvious later—he was lazy. His first day, Fosse was supposed to be tending the animals. Part of that job was making sure the gate was closed after a car left the driveway. When Polly drove through the gate, Fosse was careful to find out from her that she would be back in a half hour. But Fosse wasn't about to run down to the gate twice to close it behind her and to open it on her return in so short a time span. You can guess what happened. Within minutes, the horses had jogged through the open gate and into the neighbor's cornfield.

"My God, they've broken out," Fosse shouted, puffing up the stairs. "I'm sorry. Really sorry. Now what d'we do?"

"Hey," I said, "slow down. It's no big deal. We just go get 'em." I pulled on my shoes. The rest of the boys were away at baseball practice, so it was just Fosse, me, and Moose. "C'mon," I said, and set out toward the cornfield at a fast trot, with Fosse panting at my side. As we reached the road, we saw Moose charging down the driveway after us, looking for all the world like a hippopotamus doing something out of *Swan Lake*. Moose was bellowing happily as he ran, glad for the prospect of sharing any outdoor activity.

But Fosse took it wrong. "I bet he thinks it's real funny," Fosse said sarcastically. Then he added, "I hope you won't send me back."

By this time I'd spotted the horses and felt less interested in Fosse's train of thought than in getting the animals. "C'mon," I urged and set off in a dead run. Fosse and Moose trailed behind as we headed through the corn. I didn't look around, but I knew where Fosse was from his heavy breathing. "You cut around them, and I'll start them for the road," I shouted.

For a moment Fosse didn't respond. Then, from behind me, I heard him say, "My God! I'm dying!"

I stopped and turned around. Fosse was lying on the ground in a heap. He was panting, and his skin was the color of the lake algae. "Good Lord!" I said, "What's wrong?"

"I'm dead. I'm exhausted. I haven't run this much in my life," he said, "and I can't move another step."

Moose trotted up to where Fosse sprawled on the ground. "Lazy turkey!" he observed accurately.

Together, Moose and I grabbed the horses which were enjoying their fill of the forbidden corn. When we brought them past Fosse, we lifted him atop Giz, my big roan, and headed for the house. Fosse didn't say a word.

Moose went into the house, and while I walked the horses to the barn, Fosse slowly came back to life. "I gotta get in shape," he said.

"Really!" I agreed.

"This place will kill me."

"You'll put on thirty pounds in a year, and you'll be able to cross a street without having apoplexy."

We walked up to the house without saying anything more, but just before we went inside, Fosse unloaded something that had been on his mind. "He didn't have to enjoy my mistake so much," remarked Fosse, referring to Moose.

I wondered if I should correct his impression of Moose. Moose doesn't hold grudges; he doesn't stay mad at people from one moment to the next. He just calls them like he sees them. I decided to let Fosse figure Moose out for himself.

"I didn't know you cared what people thought of you," I said. "Maybe you aren't as dumb as you act. One thing for sure, though, Fosse, you had better watch the horses more closely. They already have you figured as lazy on the gate. You watch them when they hear a car motor. They'll start sliding toward the gate with the taste of fresh corn in their mouths."

Fosse looked at me like he thought I was kidding.

"Don't take my word for it, man," I said laughing. "Just don't call me the next time you let the horses escape."

The going was tough for Fosse from time to time, but he was quick to pick up with the rest of the boys. He seemed to be learning from each incident, even though he came close to getting his nose bent a few times.

Then one morning a few weeks later, I came down to an unusually quiet kitchen even though the boys were all there. I sat down, stirred some sugar into my coffee, and waited.

Michael finally broke the silence. At thirteen Michael was big for his age. Fortunately, he was slow to boil, but when he did get hot, he cleared an area like a tornado. No one messed with Michael.

"I'm short four dollars and fifty cents," he said, "and Fosse seems to have a new carton of cigs hidden under his pillow."

Fosse turned to me. "Dr. Oden," he protested self-righteously, "no one's supposed to search my things without my personal permission. That violates my rights."

Slurp.

Michael smiled sweetly at Fosse. Then he came angrily to the point. "Now, if I don't get some money back, and an I.O.U. for the rest," he said to Fosse, "you are either going to get your face rearranged or get thrown out of the house on your ass!"

"Watch your mouth, Michael," I snapped.

"Sorry, Dad," Michael said. "I don't know which it'll be; I'm too mad now to decide."

"You can't lay a hand on me," Fosse sputtered. "That's assault—aggravated assault, and I'll sue this place. I'll have you working for me for the rest of your life."

I didn't look up. Fosse knew his way around a foster home. He was like a little matador, taunting the bull with legal footwork. I wondered if Fosse was smart enough to realize, however, that this bull would just charge him down.

"Who knows . . . a horse might kick you," Michael shrugged at the rest of the boys. "Or you might get careless and fall out of bed. A bale of hay might fall off the pile and squash you. We've got ways. . . ."

There was a long silence. Everyone watched Fosse. Was he going to challenge Michael? Really now! But Fosse had an uncanny instinct for knowing how far he could push a person. After Michael began to storm, Fosse looked down and ate quietly, glancing at me to see if I would interfere.

Slurp.

Fosse was looking toward the wrong person for an ally. The boys were all angry at Fosse because he had violated a basic rule around the house: to respect the property of others.

Just then Moose stood up. Moose wasn't concerned with Fosse's theft of Michael's money. What Moose saw was a grosser violation of fair play. He stomped his foot and looked sternly at Michael. "He's too small," Moose bellowed, "you big fat bully!"

Michael looked at Moose. Moose glared back at Michael, shaking his finger at him. Finally, Michael turned back to Fosse. "You owe me, man," he said, "and I won't forget." The rest of the boys dug into their food. Then Moose laughed out loud and came over to me. "Give me a kiss," he said. When things get tense, Moose wants a little reassurance.

Again I wondered if Fosse was reading Moose. Moose had just stood up for Fosse. But I was sure from the scowl on his face, that Fosse thought Moose was making fun of his size and requesting affection from me that Fosse had no access to.

The incident was forgotten when Fosse repaid Michael and began to fully participate in our family. He watched the boys play foosball and one-on-one basketball, and though he didn't win for a month, he worked at it. Soon he was beating them all. He taught the boys some new moves in chess and how to play cribbage. The longer he stayed, the more he began to get it together. But he was still leery of Moose.

Fosse began to do his chores without complaint, and I only had to catch him sneaking smokes twice before he quit. He even took up ballet. At first it was a put-on for my benefit, but as he got into it, he really took a liking to it. Then, when he learned that he could take band if he maintained a passing average, he even began attending school regularly. It was his interest in band that led to a very important development at home.

Fosse had been given an old set of drums by the high school band instructor, and when he was frustrated or angry, he'd set them up in the workroom behind the garage and give them hell. What none of us realized was that Moose had become fascinated with the drums and often listened outside the workroom as Fosse banged away.

One day Moose followed Fosse into the workroom. Fosse had just set up for a session and looked up to see Moose blocking the doorway. As usual, Fosse misunderstood Moose's intentions. He thought Moose was after him. "Now look, man," Fosse said as he glanced about desperately for a door or window, "I've got something in here that will make you happy. Very happy." Fosse babbled on as he rummaged in his snare drum carrying case.

Moose stared at him for a few moments and then stomped his foot. "Shut up!" Moose bellowed.

Fosse froze. It was the first thing Moose had said that Fosse understood for sure. Then Moose pointed to the drums. "Poun'," he demanded.

Fosse was still more concerned with surviving than with listening to Moose. "Now look, ol' buddy . . ." He poured on the syrup.

Moose was getting frustrated at not being understood. "Gothdammit, I mad!" he said.

Fosse leaped behind the drums and tried to crouch out of sight.

"Shit," Moose bellowed, stomping his foot. He picked up the wooden handle of a pick ax that was on hand and took aim at the bass drum.

"Wait, wait," Fosse yelled, flagging at Moose with his hands. "Don't get mad. That thing cost a lot of bread, man, and I'm signed out for it."

Fosse's drum sticks were jutting out of his pocket, and Moose snatched them in a quick motion. Fosse interpreted the move wrongly again, and began backing away from Moose, fear gripping him.

By this time, Moose's patience had worn through. "Gothammit," he screamed. "Sit!" He put the sticks to Fosse's chest and, with a little shove, sat Fosse down against his will.

Now, with Fosse seated in playing position, Moose held out the sticks and smiled for the first time. "Poun'." he insisted.

Fosse carefully took the sticks from Moose. He tapped at the snare as if to see if the encounter had affected his touch. He sneaked a look to see where Moose was and took a caper through the cymbals and bass. Moose was now grinning down at him in admiration.

Finally, Fosse began to tumble. "You like drums!"

he said incredulously. Again he ran a number on the snare and quickly looked up at Moose. Moose stood there, mouth hanging open, eyes twinkling behind the three inches of glass. Fosse began to relax. "Hey, man, check this out." Fosse beat out a quick rhythm and Moose tip-toed around in a circle ecstatically. "Moose, you old hep cat!" Fosse laughed. Fosse gave a rap, watching Moose's reaction. "You really dig drums, don't you?" Then Fosse snapped his fingers. "You want to try?"

Moose took the sticks and looked at them.

"Come on," Fosse said, "give them a lick." Moose took a swipe at the snare with one of the sticks and completely missed. "That's okay," Fosse slapped his arm enthusiastically. "Try again, Moose."

This time Moose connected, and he jumped up and down, clapping his hands. "Now, look," Fosse said, "basically, drums are just a change in speed." Fosse took Moose's big mitts in his, struck a couple of fast beats and then one tap followed by a pause. "That's the idea."

They both stood there and grinned at each other.

Two hours later Fosse and Moose emerged. Fosse, just barely able to maintain a sober expression, dragged me downstairs to the workroom. "Moose," he said, "give me a perididdle."

Without saying a word, Moose picked up the sticks.

Bum biddle de bum.

"Now a double perididdle."

Bum biddle de biddle de bum.

"Now a double with the cymbal."

Bum biddle de biddle de bum. SMASH.

Moose stood at attention. Then he lifted his chin as high as he could and let out his high pitched laugh of pure delight. He was extremely proud of himself.

Fosse turned to me. "Well, you know what they say, man."

I just stood there, shaking my head.

"All blacks got rhythm," we said together.

* * *

Fosse had never met a person who was as open and straightforward as Moose. He kept looking for catches or exceptions. When he didn't find any, Fosse became Moose's friend and protector.

One evening we were at a basketball game in which Biddy, Michael, Markel, and Eric were playing. When we go to the games, Moose doesn't like to sit still, so we've learned to let him wander around the stands. More than once he has been known to end up at the hot dog stand. On these occasions Fosse or one of the other boys will trail after Moose.

On this night, Moose and Fosse were wandering along the sidelines during half time when a young high school student noticed Moose and began staring at him.

I really don't know what goes through Moose's head when people stare at him. At any rate, Moose grinned at this kid. "Turkey," Moose volunteered in a friendly way.

The kid stopped in his tracks. "You talkin' to me?"

"Big turkey," Moose said, "you big cow."

The youth stopped and glared at Moose. "Hey, punk, no nigger calls me 'turkey'." With that, the boy dropped his jacket to the floor and moved menacingly toward Moose.

Quick as a cobra, Fosse jumped between Moose and the boy. "Cool it, man," Fosse said.

The kid started to sweep Fosse aside. "No nigger calls me names."

"Listen, turkey," Fosse said loudly, "if you want a piece of somebody, you get me first. Turkey. You hear me, turkey? I'm calling you a turkey. What are you going to do about it, turkey?"

The boy looked at Fosse. There was fire in Fosse's eyes and a tone that shouted discretion would be the better part of valor. The kid backed off.

Fosse immediately broke into that easy grin of his. "Hey," he said, "you've got class, pal. You know when to stop. I'm Foster Johnson," he said, sticking out his hand.

"Tom," replied the kid, shaking hands. They began to talk.

"I want you to meet my pal, Moose," Fosse said. "But you gotta understand one thing. Moose only calls people he likes 'turkey'."

"You're putting me on," said Tom, looking at Moose. From the questions in his eyes, it was clear he still had some reservations. But he stuck out his hand. "Hey, turkey, glad to know you," Tom said with a chuckle. Moose took Tom's hand and gave it a hearty shake.

"Moose is retarded," said Fosse.

"Me not 'tarded," shrieked Moose.

"I get the picture," Tom said softly. "I should have guessed. I thought something was different when I first saw him. Hey, man, I'm really sorry."

Fosse and Moose were a strange match, and I didn't pretend to understand it. Perhaps Moose found in Fosse someone who took him seriously, and maybe Fosse finally discovered that he could get Moose to do things that no one else would even think of trying. In any case, Fosse had discovered a part of Moose that we hadn't known. Their unusual match-up brought some things out about each of them that we never would have suspected.

On the ground floor of the house was a television set for the boys. Fosse liked to watch TV. That's really an understatement—Fosse would watch three television sets at once if he had them. Having the one, he would watch one channel till the commercial came on and then switch to another, and so on, keeping a line on two or three channels at one time.

Moose was addicted to horror movies. Godzilla, Frankenstein, Rodan, and the Monster from the Deep Lagoon were Moose's heroes. So Fosse and Moose spent a lot of time together in front of the TV.

I was observing Moose and Fosse in front of the tube one day when I almost heard the wheels turn in Fosse's head. Seemingly out of the blue, Fosse held up four fingers. "Moose," he said, "what number is this?"

Moose looked at Fosse like Fosse had lost his marbles.

"Look, Moose," Fosse said, "you go to school. You been going eight years. Now don't give me any crap about not knowing your numbers."

"Phooey!"

Fosse sat upright in his chair. "You big fat turkey!" Moose grinned.

"You've been coasting for eight years, Moose, and now it's gotta stop!" Fosse went upstairs into the kitchen and quickly returned. He held up a hand full of raisins.

Moose's eyes got big as eggplants. "Raisin!" he said, getting up from his chair.

Fosse put up a hand. "Sit," he said, "it's a game. You tell me how many raisins I'm holding up, and you can eat them."

"Raisin," Moose repeated, ignoring Fosse, "mmmmmmm."

"Hey, Moose. You can give that to the teachers at school, but this is me, your ol' buddy, Fosse. Now tell me, how many raisins is this?" Fosse held up one raisin. He waited a minute, but got nothing from Moose. "Okay, say 'one,' Moose."

Moose gazed steadily at the handful of raisins. A little river had begun to run down the side of his mouth. Patiently, Moose waited.

"Moose," Fosse said, "first say something."

Moose smiled. "Pease."

Fosse sighed. "No, Moose. You have to say more than 'please.' You have to say, 'one.'"

"Pease, one," Moose tried.

"Beautiful, beautiful," Fosse jumped up and slapped Moose on the back and hugged him. "Now if you want more raisins, you can ask for them by numbers. See, if you want two, you can say, 'give me two, please.'"

Moose was into it by now. "Pease, all."

Fosse's motivation for the lesson soon became apparent. Three days later, the two of them were sitting before the tube, and a commercial came on. "Gimme channel four," Fosse said.

Moose approached the set and took off his glasses. He lowered his head until his nose was within inches of the knob. He squinted at the numbers; then he clicked the dial to four.

"Good," Fosse said. He watched a moment, and then became restless. "Now channel five."

Moose squinted again. Click.

"Good, Moose," Fosse said. He watched a moment and cocked his head. Then he looked sour. "Now let's try channel nine," Fosse said, in his constant search for variety.

Click, click, click, click.

I watched until I was sure of what I was seeing; no matter what sequence Fosse asked for, Moose switched the dial in the fewest number of clicks. Fosse, in all his laziness, had taught Moose the numbers from one to thirteen and the relationships between them. I sat a moment, stunned. I wondered what Fosse and Moose could do with a hundred channels!

I puzzled over this for several days and finally had

to go to Moose's school and ask. If Fosse could teach
Moose math, why couldn't they? Well . . . his teachers
said that many people like Moose couldn't add and
subtract, so they hadn't risked frustrating him by trying to
teach it. Then they said they weren't sure that learning
math would be of any value to Moose anyway, except for
changing TV channels, and that wasn't the sort of thing
they thought school was for. I questioned their reasons
for not teaching Moose numbers. I knew that Moose
didn't learn what he didn't want to learn. But I now knew
that Moose could learn numbers, and learn them in a very
functional way. I wondered idly if Fosse could teach
Moose to read, too.

* * *

Fosse and Moose. What a pair!
One night we were at the county fair, looking at
some homemaking exhibits when Moose grabbed my
sleeve. "Come, come, Daddy," he said. I guess I tried to
ignore him and continued to talk to Polly about the
exhibits. "Come, pease," Moose implored.
He guided me to a booth where a woman was
making halloween costumes. She had sewn a black velvet
suit and a flowing silk cape, and a man next to her was
modeling it. His face was neatly painted so that he looked
like Moose's friend from Transylvania.
"Fosse's daddy," Moose chortled.
"No, Moose. That's not Fosse's daddy. That's
Dracula. Be nice to the man," I teased, "or he'll bite your
neck. He'll turn you into a vampire!"
Moose threw back his head and laughed. "Fosse's
daddy," he said, "that Fosse's daddy."
Dracula looked at us strangely. "I'm not anybody's
daddy," Dracula informed us. "Really, I have a
niece . . . but she's in Idaho."
Fosse wasn't far away. I found him and asked him
what was going on. "Oh," he grinned, "once when we
were watching late TV, I told him Dracula was my father.
You do see a family resemblance, don't you?"
I gave Fosse the fish eye. "If you don't start eating
more meat, Fosse," I said, "you'll need a pint of fresh
blood. But that's about the only resemblance I see."
It was an interesting lesson to me. Moose had
remembered Fosse's statement and associated it with a
later experience.

Moose and Fosse were now laughing about the "joke" they shared. I scratched my head, trying to put this together with what I'd heard or read about the thinking capacities of people with Down's syndrome.

Fosse's continued success with Moose began to convince me that that information wasn't entirely accurate. I decided to encourage Fosse to teach Moose as much as he could.

The boys were sitting around on the kitchen stools the next morning, noses into their books, doing homework. Moose was peering over Fosse's shoulder, asking questions. Fosse had had enough of Moose. "Hey, you old turkey, don't you know? I gotta finish this, or your daddy will hang me up by my heels."

Moose stomped. "Shit." He stormed around the room, turned the radio on so loud all the boys got on him, and muttered unintelligible things to everyone, especially Fosse.

Fosse finished a chapter, looked up at the scene, and laughed. "Hey, Moose, of course you're mad! Everyone around here's got a book and you don't!" Fosse found a *National Geographic* and gave it to Moose. "Here, sit beside me and do your work."

Moose was delighted.

"And keep your fat mouth shut!" Fosse added.

I watched Moose thumb through the magazine. "Why don't you teach him to read and to write his name?" I suggested to Fosse.

Fosse looked introspective; then his eyes gleamed. I was sure the raisins would appear, and that the chalk, blackboard, and dictionary would end up in Fosse's room. But it wasn't until later, when Moose came to me with a pencil and a paper, that I realized Fosse hadn't lost his capacity for a joke. First Moose scribbled out a very shaky M-o-o-s-e. "Me," he said, pounding on his chest, "Moose."

"Hey, that's neat," I said. "You did it. You really spelled your name. That's great! Let me give you a big hug and kiss."

"En oh," he said, spelling out the word *no*. I drew back. I'd never, but *never* been refused a hug and kiss. "How about some chips then?"

Again he beamed. "En oh—yes."

"You sick, Moose? When do you start turning down junk food?"

Fosse came in, grinning mischievously. "You want a punch in the nose, Moose?"

Moose cracked wide. "Wy ee ess. No."

"You can sure spell," Fosse said, chuckling. "You want a glass of water?"

"En oh," Moose said.

"Me, too," Fosse said, "why don't you get two and put ice in mine."

Moose headed for the kitchen, proud of his academic performance. Fosse started to go, too.

"Ah, Fosse," I said. He could tell from my tone of voice that something was coming, and he tried to act as if he hadn't heard me. "You keep walking away from me, you better make it fast!" I hollered. "Otherwise I'm gonna put you on the other side of that wall. Without the help of a door!"

Fosse stopped. "Yes sir?" he said, innocently.

"You taught Moose how to spell?"

"Yes, sir," Fosse said. "It ain't easy."

"Don't give me that simple act of yours, Fosse. And don't say 'ain't'."

"Yes, sir. You know how Moose gets things mixed up."

"Fosse," I said, "let's get this straight. I saw Moose and heard him spelling *yes* and *no*. He wasn't a bit mixed up." I smiled thinly at Fosse. "He simply had them backwards!"

Fosse didn't have to answer me. Moose came in with two tumblers of water, one with ice cubes. He delivered the clinking one and straddled a stool.

"You did a nice job, Moose," I said, giving Fosse a sidelong glance, "learning what Fosse taught you. You'll get some chips, 'en oh'," I said, trying to imitate him.

Moose grinned and picked up a pencil. In a very shaky hand, he carefully printed an S followed by H, followed by I, and finally T.

"Moose," I said evenly, "what does that spell?"

Moose threw his head back and laughed his ear-rending laugh. "I forget," he said.

"Moose," I repeated, "you don't forget your favorite word! Now what does that spell?"

Moose giggled and stared directly at me. I'm really glad Polly wasn't home then. And I'm even more glad that we didn't have a house full of people, which is often the case, because I caught myself shouting at Moose, "what does s-h-i-t spell?"

Moose looked at Fosse and giggled. "Do-do," he said, and they broke up laughing.

I try to keep four-letter words to a minimum in my house, because I want the boys to learn to express themselves in other ways. But I must admit, I cracked up as much as the boys this time. Knowing Fosse and his sense of humor, I wonder just how many such words he'd have taught Moose, and in how many languages, if I hadn't caught him.

Fosse Johnson was right. He did get into the heads of the boys. He certainly got into my head. And he got into Moose's head in ways that the rest of us thought impossible.

Fosse doesn't live with us anymore, but he still drops by the house from time to time. The other day I asked him what he was going to do after he finished high school.

"Who said I was going to finish high school?" he snapped without hesitation. Fast and smooth, that's Fosse. But I've seen his reports, B's and occasional A's.

The first thing Fosse does when he visits is walk up to Moose. "Come on, man, give me a single."

Moose holds out his two huge hands and struggles to snap his pudgy fingers. Snap snapple de snap.

"Now a double."

Snap snapple de snapple de snap.

"Who's my daddy, Moose?"

And Moose throws one arm up, parallel to the ground, hiding all of his face except his eyes. He forms a claw with his other hand and holds it out menacingly. He dances his Transylvania waltz, and he and Fosse break up laughing.

CHAPTER NINE

What do you expect of your cherished offspring as they grow up and mature? You may think of college or you may wonder about your child's eventual marriage and family. You may hope your child will be popular, or smart, or perhaps a gifted skater or pianist. There is really no end to what you might imagine for your children, if they are normal. I know; I have such hopes for ten of mine. But I have an eleventh, and he's the one I really wonder about.

In the first place, we consider ourselves lucky that Moose has lived into adolescence and is still healthy. But beyond that, we really haven't known what to expect. A lot of the horrors we had anticipated haven't occurred. But what should we look forward to? Will he learn to cook? Will he ever have a hobby? What sorts of skills will he be able to develop? Will he have lasting friends? Early in his life, we were told to expect very little. But time after time, Moose has surprised us.

In the hard, cold world of adults and competitive children, Moose has done okay. He's learned how to take his lumps. He can take teasing and not let it get to him. He can handle being pushed to the end of the line. He can have something on the tip of his tongue and still wait while the fast mouths get out what they want to say first. That's the world he's accustomed to, and we are pretty happy with his progress in it.

So we got to thinking. Why not celebrate that progress.

Moose's sixteenth birthday was coming up, and we decided to have a "real" birthday party for him and invite his friends.

When we asked Moose if he wanted a party, his eyes got big behind his thick plate glass windows. He started naming the kids he wanted to invite. He made it very clear he wanted strawberry ice cream, chocolate ice cream, chocolate cake, and cookies. Then he thought for a minute, sucked on his thumb, and looked up as he had another bright idea. "Chips!" he added. "I want chips!"

Polly called the school with what we considered a simple request. She wanted a list of the phone numbers of the parents of the other students in Moose's special education class. The secretary was surprised. She'd never had such a request before. At first she informed Polly that it might be an invasion of privacy, or possibly against the law. Finally, the principal talked to Polly, asking what we were going to do with the list.

"We're having a birthday party for Moose," Polly explained. There was a long silence at the other end. "Are you there?" Polly asked.

"Oh, yes," the principal's voice said. "You said you were, ah. . . ."

"Having a birthday party. For Moose."

"Oh yes. Of course." More silence.

Then Polly said, "If you'll just give me the names, I'll be happy to look them up in the phone book."

"That might be better," the principal said.

When Polly hung up, she related the conversation to me. We wondered, Didn't the parents interact with each other? Actually, *we* hadn't, so it was reasonable to guess that the others didn't either. We shrugged and reached for the phone book.

Polly and I began making telephone calls to the parents of the other students in Moose's class.

We learned that our invitation was bound to be followed by stunned silence. The parents of Moose's best friend, Corky Mattson, were typical. Mrs. Mattson answered the phone and listened to my invitation. There was a long pause.

"Mrs. Mattson?"

"You want Corky to come to your house for a party?" Her tone was incredulous, and I thought for a moment she was going to hang up on me.

"I thought we'd start after lunch and end around four."

Mrs. Mattson still sounded shocked. "You want me and my husband to come over and 'watch' him?"

"Not really," I said. "You're welcome to stay if you like, but you don't need to."

"Really?" Another long silence while she conferred with someone. After a moment, she came back on the line. "You mean you and your wife are going to handle that whole class by yourselves?"

"It's not a big deal," I said.

"Well," she said, "Corky can come, but I don't know if we'll just *leave* him with you. It's the first birthday party he's ever been to, and I'm not sure how he'll take to it."

Most of the other parents we talked to thought we were crazy for even suggesting that all the kids come over without every parent standing by. Their kids had never been to a birthday party outside their own homes, and they were worried about how their children might behave. In one way or another, all the parents reserved the right to come over and observe the activities. I was interested in their reactions, because I'm sure that parents of normal children wouldn't have given such an invitation another thought.

When I took Moose to the store to pick out the ice cream and cake, he reminded me that we would need lots of soda and plenty of chips. I thought a large sack of chips would be sufficient, but Moose wanted three, so I bought three. Afterwards, we went to the bakery to look at some of their cakes. We decided on a big, square, double-decked, lemon-flavored cake with chocolate frosting, and we described how we wanted it decorated. Moose wanted to take the cake right then. I explained that we would come back and pick it up the next day after the bakers had time to bake and decorate it. Moose didn't answer. But when we got home, he leaped out of the car and made a beeline for Polly.

"Momma," Moose said, "daddy forgot cake." By the time I came upstairs with the soda he was in a small rage.

"Thwee bag chips and daddy mad. So no cake!" Polly asked me what it was about. Apparently, Moose thought that by getting me to buy three bags of chips, he had been bargained out of the cake. I tried again to explain to him that we would pick up the cake tomorrow, but he was still pretty hot about it and muttered to himself.

Polly smiled. "You'll have your cake, Moose. You'll have your cake."

Moose smiled back. He started getting out the cake dishes.

"No, no," Polly said. "You and your daddy will pick it up tomorrow when he comes home from work."

Moose continued to glare at me, thinking I might have pulled one over on both him and Polly. He picked up some scraps of paper and twisted them between his thumb and forefinger. I'd seen him do that before the same way. But now he spied a long tangled piece of clear plastic wrapping paper. Moose twirled the plastic a few times into a long, string-like toy. His eyes began to glow with wonder as the patterns sparkled in the light. Moose pin-wheeled the paper around in a circle. He was transfixed. He snatched another piece of loose paper and tied it to the first one like a leash. Now he twirled the thing in the air, thoroughly pleased with himself. For a long while, he studied the shadows of the whirling toy on the wall.

I guess I was as fascinated with Moose's new toy as he was. "Watcha got?" I asked.

Moose looked at me, then back at the cellophane. "Like a to'nado," he said.

I looked. I saw no tornado. I shrugged. "That's a neat . . . thing," I said. "You made yourself a toy, Moose. A sort of a . . . thing."

Moose spun his thing and sucked his thumb. He was still pouting. But now he had company to pout with. He and his thing pouted at me with great intensity.

"Moose!" I said in my most authoritative tone, "you're going to get your damned cake." He turned his head half around, and looked at me sidelong.

"Fluffle de floufle?"

"Take your thumb out of your mouth when you talk to me," I said.

"Lemon and chocolate?" he repeated.

"Yes, Moose. It will be lemon cake with chocolate frosting. And decorated, you big fat turkey!"

Moose's eyes sparkled. Then he turned his face to

the wall and sucked furiously on his thumb. "''Anks,
daddy."

The guests started arriving at around one o'clock
on Saturday afternoon. First to arrive was Corky Mattson,
carrying a large, brightly-papered box. His father and
mother trailed behind, pretending to engage in
conversation and to pay no attention to Corky. Yet their
frequent glances in his direction belied their apparent lack
of concern. Corky, a birth-trauma victim without visible
physical anomalies, was grinning from ear to ear. His
mother, in a tailor-made, silk pantsuit and fur coat,
followed, flanked by his father, in suit and tie. Corky was
wearing a parka over his sweat shirt, which he'd already
soiled, and a pair of Levis. His huge paunch hung over
his belt. Corky danced up to the house, chanting a
greeting, "Big, fat, Moose, I'm going to knock you loose."
He giggled each time he chanted it, then broke into the
same singsong phrase. He was drooling a bit, and his
nose was running, but he looked great to Moose, whose
face lit up when he saw Corky.

I'm not sure where Moose discovered his manners,
for his hosting style was certainly not like either Polly's or
mine. At any rate, he stood at the door, wearing a
brand-new jumpsuit he had persuaded his mother to
make him and a cap (freshly starched at his insistence)
that looked very similar to a railroad engineer's. He
swung the door open and hollered out greetings at the
top of his lungs. "Corky Mattson, thud row fum the left,
thud seat. Hi, Corky, come on in." Then he spotted Mrs.
Mattson and Mr. Mattson, and stage fright suddenly
overtook him. He looked at the ground shyly. Then he
raised his head and boomed out, "Mr. Corky and Mrs.
Corky, please come in and make y'self t'my home."
Stepping back with a bow and a great sweeping motion of
his arm, he waved them grandly into his house. Moose
brought the Mattsons upstairs to the living room and
repeated his performance for Polly and myself.

Corky stood subdued in the center of our huge
living room, looking rather uncomfortable in the new
surroundings. Moose went over to him, not knowing
quite what to do next. At first, he sucked on his thumb
and looked at Polly and me. We looked away, letting
Moose handle his own affairs. Then Moose smiled. I think

he was glad we were letting him handle this on his own. He took Corky to the kitchen, which was just off the living room while Mr. and Mrs. Mattson watched.

"Dis da kitchen," Moose began. "Here's da icebox." He opened the door and pointed to things inside. "See? Cheese, milk, icebox." He closed the door, then went to the stove and pointed to it. "Dis da stove," he said, twisting the buttons on the front of it. "Dese buttons make on and off." He then went to the sink and detailed its function along with the rest of the items in the kitchen. I watched, thinking that Moose certainly knew what his priorities were. He spent about fifteen minutes in the kitchen, one minute in the bedroom, and three minutes in the bathroom. Then he and Corky went outside to look at the animals.

I turned to Mr. and Mrs. Mattson, and smiled. "Moose certainly knows how to give a tour. Sort of like us . . . Moose shows off what he's interested in."

Mr. and Mrs. Mattson nodded and looked for a place to sit.

"You really don't have to stay," I said. "The boys can take care of themselves." I indicated the teen-agers standing by. "And we have plenty of help. You can certainly stay if you like though." The Mattsons sat down on the couch. They had no intention of leaving their son. "Y'know," I said, "I hope we can all relax and enjoy the party. Let the kids do their thing. Can't ruin the house. Everything scrubs up. Okay?"

By this time another car had arrived, and Moose left the animals to greet the Withers. Jamie Withers was a young girl of about sixteen whose physical appearance had been affected by considerable birth injuries.

"Hi, Jamie," Moose said, half dragging her out of the car by her arm. He was long on enthusiasm and a little short on finesse. Her parents leaped out of the car, quickly extricating their daughter from Moose's energetic grasp. Undaunted, Moose smiled broadly at them. "Hello, Mr. and Mrs. Jamie," Moose said. "You want to come where Mommy is."

Moose had no sooner completed his introductions and shown Jamie the house, when three more cars pulled up.

Johnny Joseph jumped out of his parents' car almost before it had stopped and ran around in circles on

his short, bowed legs. He was shouting at the top of his
lungs, apparently trying to imitate an early and energetic
Elvis Presley and beating his chest like Tarzan. He was in
open delight at the fact that Pixie Talbot had just arrived.
Racing over to her car, he nearly ripped the door off in his
desire to reach her.

Pixie was a cute girl, with a roundish face and a
little, turned-up nose, so it was a bit surprising when her
slow, dull speech and difficult articulation revealed she
was retarded. She stepped out of the car, somewhat shy
at Johnny's show of pleasure.

Bob Thompson was helped out of the car and into
his wheelchair by his parents. He had been a carbon-
monoxide victim as a youngster. He was very thin
and his eyes were crossed upwards, giving him a
prayerful appearance and earning him the nickname
"minister." The children pronounced it "minster," and
that was the name that stuck.

Johnny Joseph bounded over, enthusiastically
trying to help Mr. Thompson wheel Minster up to the
door. Johnny's efforts nearly tipped over the wheelchair.
To this, Minster giggled nervously and his eyes unlocked
from their angelic expression long enough to reflect the
fear that he might be dumped on his nose.

As the procession neared the house, Moose went
into his routine, announcing everyone and then leading
the entourage up the steps and into the living room.
Moose repeated his tour of the house with Corky filling in
any missing details. Jamie also knew things about the
kitchen that Moose didn't, so open arguments broke out
about whether or not the stove was gas or "'lectric," and
whether we had an "ice box" or "'frigerator."

We were waiting for Danny Brighton, when his
mother called to say that Danny had stolen the keys to a
schoolbus and that she would have to drop them off
before their arrival.

We were all gathered in our large dining room,
waiting for them and watching as Moose made the last of
his introductions. The parents were a little uneasy but
were attempting to make conversation with one another.
The Withers, for example, admitted that this was the first
time that Jamie had been to a party "in public" and
acknowledged that they really appreciated the invitation.
They explained that Jamie had two brothers and

three sisters, each of whom had had birthday parties, but the Withers hadn't quite known how to handle Jamie's birthday. "We don't mind having 'regular' birthday parties at our house or sending our children to other 'regular' birthday parties. But Jamie is not 'regular,'" said Mr. Withers.

And Mrs. Withers added, "We just have a family picnic or an ice-cream treat at home, where people won't be upset by Jamie's coordination problems."

Jamie had never asked why she could not have a party; she just "knew"! Nobody in the family really wanted to talk about that embarrassing issue. Both Mr. and Mrs. Withers commended us for giving Moose this party.

Gradually, the other parents loosened up and began to reflect the same sentiments. All of the adults came to agree that these parties *should* happen. "After all," one commented, "our handicapped children are entitled to the same kinds of experiences as other children."

Each was able to relate frustrations they had had trying to treat their children normally. They began to laugh at themselves, at being uptight when their children drooled, misspoke, or spilled. "We really shouldn't let it bother us," one parent said, "that our children have small problems with inconsequential things such as blowing their noses or putting their shirts on straight."

I sighed. "Yeah, I feel the same way. And I guess I'm a little embarrassed at not really letting Moose enjoy the kind of life our other boys have just because of my own fears."

One of the parents suggested, "Let's make a pact among ourselves that we will provide our children with the kinds of experiences other children enjoy."

The other parents nodded their agreement.

Our resolutions were broken up by the arrival of Danny "Fingers" Brighton in a Lincoln Continental.

Danny stepped out of the car, looking like he owned the world. He was a handsome seventeen-year-old who was only mildly retarded.

Quickly Danny went around to the driver's side to open the door for his mother. "Thank you, my dear," she cooed and patted him on the cheek. Then she turned to the house and took Danny's arm. He was dressed expensively in a wool coat, dark blue slacks, and cashmere sweater.

Again, Moose went into action. "Fingers and Mama Fingers, dis my doctor daddy," he announced solemnly.

Danny stuck out a big, square fist and pumped my hand as if he were drawing water. "Hi, Doc," he said, "I got this sharp thing in my back. Do you think I need some kind of medicine?"

"He's not that kind of a doctor," Mrs. Brighton said. "And keep your hands to yourself while you're here," she whispered. She leaned towards me. "Danny only steals things from people he likes," she confided. (I hoped he wouldn't like us too much.) "I'm afraid I can't stay," she added.

"I'd be glad to bring Danny home after the party," I offered.

"Would you? How nice!" she replied. "Well, good luck with your party." She raised an eyebrow as she looked over our group. "And thanks for keeping an eye on Danny. His father and I are *so* busy. . . ."

With all of the guests present, it seemed like the time to get this party off formally. Each of them had brought a gift for Moose and laid it on the counter in the kitchen. I looked from the stack of presents to Moose and suggested that he might want to open them so that everybody could find out what the surprises were. Corky Mattson, seeing what was up, rushed over to his gift. He grabbed it in both hands, ran toward Moose, and stopped in front of him. Then, before his aghast parents could stop him, he began to tear the wrappings from it. Horrified at his manners, Mrs. Mattson hurried quickly over, took the package from Corky, and chided him. As if by signal, the rest of the parents fell upon the packages, giving their children instructions in tones that were low, but unmistakably authoritarian.

For just a moment, I wanted to rush in and help Moose, too. But the image of all the parents helping their children to "act right" stopped me short. Why should we be helping Moose and his friends? It was their party, and it would remain that. "Hey, folks," I said, "the kids are doing fine by themselves. They don't need our help. Who'll join me in a glass of wine instead?"

The parents looked from one to another. Slowly, they realized that they had fallen into that trap we'd been talking about earlier. They dropped the packages and moved to the back of the room where they could watch and be out of the way. I got out goblets and poured some wine.

Corky leaped upon his package again and tore the wrappings from it, exposing a long-playing record.

"My best record," Corky said to Moose. "'Shu-ba-du.'"

Moose clapped his hands together. Corky's excitement about the gift was contagious, and Moose caught a bad case of it. Immediately, Moose placed the record on the turntable and flipped up the volume. In a few seconds, music blared from wall to wall. We had to shout to be heard.

Jamie Withers took her gift to Moose and extended it with both hands, her eyes lowered. "It isn't much," she said slowly, "and I hope you don't tear the paper. I wrapped it myself."

Moose took the gift with a simple "Thanks." He carried it over to the counter and put it down. Mrs. Withers urged him to go ahead and open it, but he stood firm. Moose stiffened his body, thrust his chin in the air, and shook his head violently from side to side. "No one gonna tear Jamie papuh," he said, and there was nothing anyone could do, including Jamie, to get him to violate the package.

Johnny Joseph fetched his package and brought it halfway to Moose. Suddenly the allure of the surprise became overwhelming, and Johnny began to tear the wrapping off himself. Johnny's present was a book about dinosaurs, a subject in which Moose was very interested. In his excitement, Johnny tore off the cover and the first few pages. Embarrassed, Mr. Joseph promised to replace it with a new book. But Moose had his thing about NOW. He found some tape and began to reassemble the book immediately. In complete concentration, Moose began to put the pages back, oblivious of their proper order. He and Johnny were both pleased with the result.

It was then time for ice cream and cake, and Moose again assumed the role of host.

Sure, Moose might make a mess. And I could have asked the other boys in the house to help. But this was. Moose's party and I had only made rules for the adults.

Moose first took plates to the parents. Apparently the adults assumed we had cake and ice cream only for the children, because they steadfastly refused any of it, in spite of the fact that it was colorful and pretty tasty. Moose, of course, was delighted, because this meant all the more for him and his pals. He took a plate and set it on Jamie Withers' lap. He then put a large slice of cake on it, and with a huge tablespoon that resembled a snow shovel more than a table implement, scooped out a large portion of ice cream and slopped it on her plate, too. The impact of the blow sent large globs of chocolate ice cream across her dress. Moose reached out with the ice cream-soaked spoon and tried to scrape it off, but only smeared it more.

I saw Mrs. Withers start to rise out of her chair, but she was restrained by her husband. I looked at her, and for an instant I saw deep embarrassment. I smiled easily, and she followed suit. They were going to experience the discomfort of "letting the kids be as they may," and try to live up to our declaration of the previous hour, in spite of reflexes to the opposite.

Corky wanted to cut his own cake and did so by slicing off a piece that barely fit on his plate, which meant that he had to put ice cream on top of the cake rather than beside it. He then dove in with both hands, forgetting there was such a thing as a fork or a spoon. Before Moose had finished serving the others, Corky had come back for a second helping, and then a third, despite the protestations of his mother, and the insistence of his father that he "only eat as much as he could handle."

When it was evident that even Corky Mattson could not exhaust the ice cream and cake supply, the parents began to join in, and Moose continued to play host. He walked over to Mrs. Withers with a large dish of chocolate ice cream and cake, and stumbled getting there, dumping the mess of cold stuff into her lap. Moose's eyes got big as he realized the blunder he had made, and he searched around the room quickly. He grabbed a dishtowel as Mrs. Withers began to stand up and attempted to wipe the large portion of melting ice cream and cake from her lap. He smeared the ice cream from her lap clear up to her bosom, leaving a broad, brown stain on her pressed, silk suit. Then, in his anxiety to clean up

the mess, Moose turned too quickly and banged Mr.
Withers' glass of wine with his elbow, knocking that
down the front of Mr. Withers' suit. Apparently oblivious
to the impact of this last blunder, Moose picked up with
his hands the mess on the floor and moved to serve the
next adult. The Withers and I exchanged looks that said
we would pay the price for our experiment in letting the
kids manage themselves, but no one moved to stop them
and the cake and ice cream were finally served.

By this time, Danny Brighton had interested Pixie
Talbot in a new game. Danny proceeded to demonstrate
at least part of the reason for his nickname. Quickly, he
pulled Pixie's dress up, and to a chorus of her
embarrassed shrieks, tried to pull her panties down.

Corky and Johnny ran into the kitchen when they
heard Pixie holler and raced around her, stomping their
feet and shouting.

"We can see, we can stare, we can see your
underwear," Corky hollered, and the rest guffawed at his
rhyme. Now Jamie came into the kitchen, just daring
Danny to repeat his game. As Danny was about to oblige,
the girls, with proper, if late, indignation raced for the
bathroom, which was hidden around the corner.

The chase that ensued resembled a scene from the
keystone cops, the girls just steps ahead of the boys.
Finally, in third spot and losing ground wheeled Minster,
no more anxious to miss the fun than anyone else. Moose
finally pulled up to a screeching halt in front of the
bathroom door. He let the girls in and put up a hand like
a cop directing traffic to a stop. "Naughty follow girls into
ba-room," he pronounced, and the chase was over.

Corky, still excited by the chase, varoomed around
the room like a vacuum cleaner, sucking up everybody's
plate and drink. By stages, his complexion turned from
rosy red to bright chartreuse, and then, in the middle of
the floor, he disgorged enough ice cream, cake, cheese,
crackers, peanuts, potato chips, punch, and two things
which looked suspiciously like cigarette butts, to form a
rather ill-smelling lake in the middle of our shag rug. His
father and mother abandoned their pledge to be
uninvolved. At once they both got up, grabbed rags and
began mopping, hopeful that they could make the lake
disappear before everybody noticed.

The record had now entered its third playing and was thumping and jumping away as loud as ever. I shouted to Mr. and Mrs. Mattson that it was all right, that we'd clean things up later. They must have forgotten that sixteen kids lived in our house so we were used to these minor catastrophes. By now, Minster had pushed his wheelchair over to the edge of the lake, and in his attempts to help clean it up, lost his balance, doing a half gainer on the way down.

Meanwhile, Mrs. Talbot had gone to the bathroom to check on Pixie. "Are you all right, honey?" she called. The silence that ensued worried Mrs. Talbot, and she gave the door a couple of raps. "Girls," she demanded, "open the door."

Now Mr. Talbot approached his wife and tried to ease her mind. "Come on, honey," he said, "she's okay. They're just playing games."

"Pixie," Mrs. Talbot said, ignoring her husband, "open the door this instant!"

Where Mrs. Talbot had little success, Johnny succeeded without even trying. He found one of Polly's old dresses in the downstairs closet and put it on. At first content to admire himself in the mirror, Johnny then minced up to Danny and flashed his skirt. Getting the reaction he wanted, Johnny gave out an ear-splitting shriek, in good imitation of the girls, and dashed off. The boys caught on to the game, screaming and giving chase. In an instant, the bathroom door popped open, and out flew the girls in a reversal of the previous chase.

Mrs. Talbot remained by the open bathroom door, shaking her head at the rapidly disappearing view of her daughter. "She doesn't *seem* upset," she said.

At last we cleaned up most of the lake, the chase ended, and the kids became absorbed in the foosball game. I turned off the record player and all of us adults experienced the first relative calm of the afternoon.

Mr. Talbot had an appointment across town, so I rounded up Pixie and saw them to the door. But they'd only been gone a few minutes when Mr. Talbot returned. "I've lost my keys," he said.

I should have known better, but I tumbled. "Oh," I said, "I'll check the closet." I went into the closet on hands and knees with a flashlight and came out five

minutes later without them. Mr. Talbot was worried that
he would miss his appointment, so I volunteered to drive
them. We would look for the keys later.

When I got back to the house, the foosball
tournament was winding down and the other parents
were preparing to leave.

I was feeling bad that the Talbots' keys had been
lost when I suddenly remembered why Fingers Brighton
had come to the party late. He was just finishing the
foosball tournament. I went to him and held out my
hand. "Come on," I said, "give me the keys." Danny
grinned sheepishly and fished out the keys which Mr.
Talbot had "lost." "Tell you what I'm going to do," I told
Danny. "*If* you promise not to steal any more keys, we'll
have lunch together sometime next week."

Danny lit up. He'd be delighted out of his socks.

"You got that? No more keys!"

Danny nodded.

Polly and I went outside with the other parents as
they began to get into their cars. They each tried to outdo
the other in thanking us. The Withers pledged to have a
party on Jamie's birthday, and other commitments to
social events for the children began to round robin. But as
the families drove off down our road, I shrugged.
"Betcha," I said to Polly, "the next party, if there is one at
all, will be right here."

Later, when I drove Danny home, I stopped by the
Talbots and explained the whole thing to Mr. Talbot.
"Y'know," I said, "Danny's mother says he only steals
from people he likes. I don't know what you did that
he likes, but could you show him some attention? I have
the feeling he doesn't get a lot. Maybe we could all get
together, with Pixie and Moose, too. We could eat out for
lunch."

"Sure, at my club," Mr. Talbot said. "I'd like to
host you. Let's check with the Brightons and make
it a date."

I think we were both glad to be making concrete
efforts to get the kids together again. When we met at Mr.
Talbot's club a few days later, Mr. Talbot immediately
shook Danny's and Moose's hands. "Hello, boys," he
said.

"Good to see you, Talbot," said Danny.

"Daddy!" said Moose. "Let's eat!"

Pixie just grinned and seemed delighted about everything.

We carefully placed Danny at one end of the table and Pixie at the other, recalling their game, but I'm not sure that was necessary or even wise. Danny was on his best behavior. Well, maybe his second best behavior. Mr. Talbot and I had a martini before lunch, and the kids had lemonade. Mr. Talbot got up to go to the lavatory, and while he was gone, Danny did away with half of his martini before I could stop him. But Mr. Talbot never knew about that. What he did know was that we had a very pleasant lunch and that the kids behaved themselves pretty well, all things considered.

I reciprocated the following week, and we didn't bother to control the seating. That way Mr. Talbot and I sat together and were able to talk a little.

I think Mr. Talbot got to like Danny. One day he said, "You've behaved really well, Danny. Kids like you really deserve better breaks than you seem to get."

I don't know if Mr. Talbot saw it or not, but ol' Moose had scooted over close to Pixie and was holding her hand under the table.

"I'll call you in a couple of weeks," I said to Mr. Talbot as we were getting up to leave.

"Yes," Mr. Talbot said, "we'll have to do this again."

I'm sure Mr. Talbot was comforted by the fact that since we had begun these lunches, Danny Brighton hadn't been known to steal anything. But as we left, I wondered how comfortable he would be about Moose and Pixie.

CHAPTER TEN

Friends and parents of retarded and handicapped children often ask me how they should relate to those children.

Some people pretend the handicap doesn't exist. That's pretty unrealistic. If a child has difficulty hearing, for example, you can't carry on a conversation as if he or she were catching everything you said. Sometimes Moose is difficult to understand. Then you have to stop and say, "Hey, I don't understand what you said." You have to remind him to speak clearly.

Other people make no demands on handicapped kids, accepting anything they do. I don't recommend that either. We sell handicapped people short when we don't expect anything of them.

I guess I've learned that you have to see each handicapped person as an individual with his or her own set of complex personal qualities. Some people do this instinctively; take Alex for instance.

I guess there aren't many people like Cadacius Alexopolus, but as I look more closely at the people I regard as my friends, I see many of them who have at least a few drops of Alex in their veins. Seeing more and more of these people maintains my overly large share of optimism.

I first met Alex when we assigned one of our foster children, Tony Brown, to his class in high school. We were having pretty good success with our foster children, partly because we expected each child in our house to take full advantage of opportunities, and we saw school as a big opportunity. Tony Brown came to us as a "last resort" before being sent to a state correction facility. He had been in and out of foster homes since he was about seven, and he had been busted for everything from theft to aggravated assault. He was a bitter kid who had been treated harshly by his foster parents and the few relatives he had. I guess you could say he had reason to be resentful.

When I told Tony that he would have to go to school, get passing marks, and stay out of trouble, he looked at me impassively, promising nothing. The only thing he agreed to do was to stay at our place for a short time to consider his options. Fortunately, Tony's teacher was Cadacius Alexopolus.

Two days after Tony started school, I got a call from Alex, who asked if I could come over and talk with him and Tony.

When I arrived, Tony was already in Alex's office. I wasn't quite sure whether Tony was dragged in by the nape of the neck, or if he came voluntarily. In either case, Tony was angry.

Alex stood in the doorway without expression, as if this was the way all students acted in school.

Alex smiled quickly as I came in, and Tony glowered back at both of us. When we were seated, Alex fixed three cups of coffee while plugging away in an animated monologue. "I guess you're wondering why I asked you to come? Glad to have you in school, Tony. You're new to the school district and you don't quite know how to take us. Maybe you're a little bit frustrated from your last school experience. How are you doing at home?

"Dr. Oden, I want you to know that he hasn't upset me yet, but I guess some of the kids and their parents are a little bit worried about him. It's funny how some people won't give another person much of a chance. I don't think Tony's a bad guy; but he sure puts up a helluva front!

"You've got a really big heart, Tony. That's what we've got to work on, your heart.

"Tony has some trouble reading, and he tries to hide the fact from everybody by playing the tough guy. Doesn't sit in his seat very long, popped a few kids during free period, and swore at the principal.

"Not much of a start at a new school, eh, Tony? But I can't really blame you for putting on a tough show in a situation you're not familiar with. Awful lot of new faces. Lots of kids acting too smart for their britches."

Alex dumped heaps of sugar and cream into one of the coffee cups and pushed it toward Tony. Tony took a couple of large sips of it and swallowed hard. Alex was still smiling at both of us and running his monologue.

"You're a neat kid, Tony, and we've got to let you find that out. Some kids you'll like, some you won't, like anywhere else. But you really can't go around busting everybody's nose. You can understand that some people get upset at that, right, Tony? As far as your school work, if you aren't ready for classes, you can take some assignments home and bring them in after school. Or we could have a tutor help you out. I could spend a couple of hours on the weekend, for example, catching you up with things, if that would help any. See, if you're scared, you can kind of warm up with some lessons outside of class, until you get used to it. Then we could put you back into the classroom."

Alex paused and faced Tony squarely. "You understand what I'm saying, Tony? It's a two-way street."

This was the second school Alex had worked in. The principal in his first school had not renewed his contract. Although liked by his students, rumor had it that Alex was just too damn much trouble for a principal. Let the long-haired weirdo do his thing elsewhere.

When Tony Brown first laid eyes on Alex, he didn't like the long-haired weirdo any better than the principal did. In three days, Tony popped Alex in the nose, slashed his car tires, and broke a window in his classroom. But to Alex, that was the surface of Tony. He was willing to look for the Tony that lay frightened underneath this tough exterior. So he worked with Tony, continually challenging him.

During the summer, Alex directed a YMCA-sponsored camp where he could work with the kids when school was out. Other counselors refused the job because they said they couldn't make ends meet on the money. But not Alex.

The first year Alex found it hard to fill his camp roster. I thought maybe I could help him and suggested that Tony Brown and Moose might attend.

I started to apologize for Moose, by saying that I had a boy who might not have the qualifications. That's all the farther I got with Alex. I should have known that would happen. Alex smiled and said, "Fine, I bet we can work with him."

I continued to protest. "He's a Down's syndrome child, and he needs a lot of supervision." Again, I got no further.

"Of course he does," Alex said. "I have some volunteer help."

Alex was going to leave it at that, but I wasn't.

"How many adults, and what is their training?" I asked. Afterward, I wondered how much like a bureaucrat I sounded, a dyed-in-the-wool member of the establishment. Still, Moose was my own son, and I was expressing general concern for his survival.

"If you will make a list of the things you want him to do, and when he should do them, we can try to accommodate you. And if you will make a list of things you don't want him to do, we'll try to prevent him from doing those, also, within reason," Alex said. I tried to look him in the eye, but all I could see was the reflection of his glasses and an occasional flash of lightning behind them. "Other than that," he said, "we'll manage to work things out for ourselves."

So we agreed that Moose and Tony would fill out the roster for Alex's summer camp. I was still a little apprehensive about sending Moose, though. It would be the first time he'd been away from Polly and me. To ease my feelings, I decided that I would stop by the camp once or twice to make sure Moose was getting along, and maybe even to see whether Alex was surviving.

With our other children, becoming independent was a natural part of growing. We loosened the reins, and they gradually began taking charge of new situations. But the forces tugging at Moose were far more subtle, and often they pulled him more closely home instead of away. Perhaps our limited expectations of him shielded him from making choices for himself. As we discussed the camp, Polly and I both tried to conceal our concerns about his safety and comfort. We wondered if he would adjust to living temporarily without us.

Moose was growing rapidly, but he was anything but an adult in my mind or Polly's. We discussed how we would send Moose off. We would drive Moose to the YMCA to meet the bus. Polly was going to hug him and kiss him, say her goodbyes, and give him some fresh fruit, a candy bar, and a comic book to look at on the bus. Then she'd dive into the car and close the door without looking back. That would be easiest on her, and Moose would not get a chance to hang on to her or cry on her shoulder and say he didn't want to go. Then it would be my turn to hug and kiss him, lead him to the bus, push him up the stairs, and wish him well.

The bus, a large van similar to ours, with "YMCA" painted on the side, tooted brightly across the parking lot. Alex waved jovially from the driver's seat. The carrier on top of the van was heaped with gear, and faces appeared at all the windows. One of the YMCA staff members helped load Moose's baggage into the back of the van. That was Polly's cue.

Moose, however, crossed us up. He walked over to Alex without a backward glance, affectionately pinched Alex's cheek, and said, "Give me a kiss." Alex leaned precariously out of the van window, kissed him on the mouth, and pulled himself back into the van. At that moment Moose turned to us, giggling shrilly. He waved goodbye and jumped into the van without further ado.

Polly and I stood there, with our candy and comic books still in hand, looking at each other. As we watched the van disappear down the road, Polly's eyes filled with tears. "It's the first time he's been away from us."

"Yeah," I said, "it appears to be tougher on us than on him."

I drove home with the good intention of doing some yard work. I hadn't worked on the fences since last fall, and there were several holes in them that needed patching badly. The fence needed painting. I had planned on sowing some alfalfa in what was now a weed patch out behind the barn, and the fenced, quarter-mile track needed dragging. Instead, Polly and I sat for awhile over coffee.

I finally managed to get out the paint bucket, the

sledgehammer, some spikes, barbed wire, and tin snips, but I was thinking so much about how Moose was getting along that I wasn't getting a great deal done. Alex had said there was a swimming pool. I wondered if it was supervised. I wondered whether Moose was lying face down in it at that moment. I wondered whether Moose might be wandering along a back trail, unable to tell his direction by the sun or the moss on the trees, unable to gain his bearings from the lay of the land. I wondered whether Moose would be able to survive in such a primitive setting away from his family. There were times when I thought Moose might be moments away from disaster.

I went back in the house. At any moment I expected the phone to ring, and I didn't want to be too far away when it did.

But the phone sat quietly on the hook.

My feet found their way to Moose's bunk and I stood before it. The springs were somewhat stretched, so it lay there like a concave bird's nest of blankets. His thing lay beside it, and one striped brown stocking hung from a chair. I was trying to remember in my mind's eye whether or not he had been wearing a pair when he left that morning.

By the side of his bed was the satchel Polly had made for him to carry his books in. I went through it absently. There were books from the previous semester, and assignments, some of Mila's calculus papers from college, and Terry's drawings. I had to admit that he had used excellent taste in selecting them. In the sack were some sketches that Earl had made of a couple of bridges across the Mississippi River in southern Minnesota. They were excellent bridges, and Moose had always been fascinated by the drawings. I also found three apples, two-and-a-half sandwiches, and a seven-ounce lump of moldy cheddar cheese. I didn't know when the food had been put into the bag, but I knew it wasn't recently. Again Moose was in my mind's eye, the flesh drawn around his cheeks, his body sallow and gaunt. Was he eating properly? Was he eating at all? Was he lost? My feet took me back to the phone, and I stood looking at it for awhile.

The camp was a sixty-minute drive out of the Twin Cities, and Alex had agreed to receive me at five o'clock.

Not before. I left at three so I would be sure to get there on time. I filled the car with gas and had some oil put in it. I drank four cups of coffee at three different stops, and finally, driving about thirty-five miles an hour down the road, *still* got there at five minutes to five.

Camp was beautifully situated off a small country road among a large stand of Norway pines. It was rolling country, divided by a creek that still flowed quite rapidly from melting snows. In the middle of the camp was the swimming pool. A make-shift springboard had been built on the side of the pool over the deepest part. On one side of the stream was a dining room and a kitchen. On the other side of the stream were two dormitory units and a large lavatory which included toilets and showers. Upstream fifteen to twenty yards was the recreation building made of roughly hewn lumber and roofed with an odd lot of shingles and tar. Further upstream from the recreation building was a large campfire area, surrounded concentrically by flat rocks. With my eyes closed, I could envision a roaring blaze, with counselors and campers sitting around it exchanging ghost stories.

The aroma of freshly boiling coffee and the sharp smell of barbecued meat and beans made my stomach come alive. There was no one in sight, though the dormitory units, standing side by side, rocked with mayhem. I walked to the doorway of one of the dorms and looked inside. There were ten boys, including Tony Brown and Moose. The other boys were of all sizes and shapes, though only Tony and Moose were black. Four or five radios were going full blast, and boys were shouting back and forth, tossing pillows at each other. Others were making up their beds with army blankets and putting clothes away in roughly-constructed lockers.

My eyes rested on Moose. He was struggling with his bed. That Moose was on the bottom bunk was encouraging. A fall from the top could hurt him, could collapse the building, and probably both. While Moose's attempts at bed-making were not examples of manual artistry, he was trying, and I couldn't ask for more.

Tony Brown was talking to his bunk mate, a boy who was a lot smaller than Tony. They were both laughing, so I backed out of the doorway before I was noticed.

There was no blood being shed, and my two boys

were accounted for. I went to the kitchen to see what was behind the smells. There I discovered Alex with three young women, peering into the fire they were using to braise the meat. They were throwing various kinds of seasonings into a huge pot. They looked up and Alex laughed.

"The concerned parent!" he said. "Glad to have you aboard. You will have supper with us." He said it like it was more than a suggestion.

"How's Moose? Everything under control?" I asked.

Alex shrugged. "Dunno," he said, "you'll have to check for yourself."

One of the women poured me a cup of coffee and I sat down. The picture of the boys making their beds came to my mind. "How in the devil did you get them to clean up their quarters so easily?" I asked.

"I simply said that nobody would eat until the beds were made and the quarters were ready." He sipped on his coffee. "Sometimes you have to look for trouble in order to find it."

One of the women rang the dinner bell. All hell broke loose then, as boys and girls spilled into the dining room and took their seats, shouting at the top of their lungs. The din was deafening.

As if by cue, Alex and his staff backed off from all the noise and began a discussion among themselves. For a full five minutes it sounded like the roof would blow off. Then Jackie Arneson, the bull of the camp with a logger's heavy shoulders, got up from his seat, went over to the counselors, and shouted even more loudly: "When the hell are we going to eat dinner?"

Alex turned around, acting surprised. He raised his eyebrows above his glasses, then cupped his ear as if he hadn't heard. Jackie screamed again, and Alex moved his mouth as if he were speaking, though no sound came out.

Jackie glared at him and put his nose half an inch away from Alex's glasses. "I can't hear a goddamn thing you're saying!" he bellowed.

Again, Alex moved his mouth as if he were speaking, and gestured in a number of complicated ways so that Jackie could not possibly understand what he was saying or doing.

Jackie turned around to the others at the table. He banged on the table until plates and flatware rattled a chorus. "Quiet down! I can't hear what the man is saying."

No one paid Jackie any attention.

For a moment, Jackie glared at the table. He went up to Tony Brown and a boy named Kurt, the two next largest boys there. He grabbed them both by the front of the shirt and lifted them out of their chairs. "You heard me say 'quiet' damn it!" he raged. "Now you two see that this table gets quiet or I'm going to smash your heads together. You got that?"

They both nodded. Jackie set them down and went back to Alex.

The hall fell silent; Jackie glowered at Alex. "Now! I said when are we gonna eat!"

Alex backed up a step. He stuck his finger in his ear. "Can you lower your voice a little?" Alex asked, a pained expression on his face.

Jackie's blood was up. He tried the same tactic which had worked with his two pals. He grabbed Alex by the collar and shook him like a rag doll. "Goddamn it," he said, "when are we going to eat and you'd better answer me now!"

I started to step in, and Alex waved me away. With Alex's glasses now at an awry position, it appeared as if his smile was tipping a little and going to fall off his face. But Alex held it there and said calmly, "For a person who wants to be fed, you're acting awfully tough. Don't you suppose you'll get further by cooperating?"

Jackie blinked at Alex, not fully realizing he still had a hold of him. Finally, Jackie released Alex and stepped back. Alex adjusted his glasses so that his smile was on straight again and addressed the group. "Oh, I see you're all ready to eat now that your before-dinner-time conversation is over." He nodded to the three staff members, who took their places in front of the food. "If you will please pick up your plates and come by the food stations, we'll serve you and you can return to your seats. Feel free to ask for seconds after you've cleaned your plates the first time."

As Jackie returned to his table, he paused by me and whispered confidentially, "I'm gonna bust that guy before this camp's over."

I started to tell him that if he touched one hair on Alex's head I'd bust him back. But then I remembered how easily Alex had handled him. I doubted that Alex needed my protection.

There began a great din as the music of flatware against tin filled the room. Four of the kids stood out: two girls, Moose, and another boy who appeared to have coordination handicaps. They ate with less than appealing grace. Moose knew what to do with a knife and fork, though his exuberance sometimes overpowered his etiquette. He cut his meat and handled his silverware as he'd seen others do. But as frustration with this process got to him, he began to pile things on his fork, so that on the way to his mouth gobs of food fell off. Still, he was making headway by the stuffed mouthfuls. It wasn't pretty, but it was effective.

Then I noticed Tillie McMahon, a girl almost six feet tall, and very slender, who had severe coordination problems. She appeared to be the victim of a serious head injury, with the scars on her face running up into her hairline. Her right arm shook uncontrollably. She contemplated the steak in front of her and looked around for help without even attempting it. I wondered if the menu had been deliberately planned to frustrate those with eating problems. But I had underestimated Alex. He signalled with his eyes for the counselors to help the kids who were having problems. One woman went to Moose and sat beside him, while Alex sat beside Tillie.

Very gently, Alex put his hands on top of Tillie's, and with her right hand, which held the knife, began to make cutting motions. When he took his hands off, she lost coordination and looked up with pleading eyes. I felt a compelling impulse to give assistance. As I began walking toward Tillie, Alex raised a hand, motioning me back. But I'd been too strongly affected by Tillie's expression. I extended my hand, as if to take her silverware and cut the meat.

Alex smiled at me. "It's nice of you to think of helping her," he said, "but she can manage by herself." Then Alex put his hand on my chest and gently pushed me back toward my seat. "After all," he said, "she's got to learn for herself, doesn't she?" I backed up a few steps and stood there, waiting to see if Alex was right and remembering the parents at Moose's birthday party.

Alex tried again, and again Tillie proved that she couldn't control the knife with her favored hand. Suddenly Alex stopped and slapped his forehead. "Of course," he muttered. He switched her knife and fork. Now she had the fork in her tremulous right hand. He helped her sink the fork deep into the steak, freeing her left hand to saw through the meat in a clean cut. Tillie looked up at Alex with surprise. Now they worked together in a cross-cut and succeeded. He just barely guided her hands in the next cut; then she made a cut on her own. She threw down the implements and shouted out with joy. "Good!" she laughed. She sat down and began sawing up the meat without eating it. Her right hand was useful, when used properly.

The counselor who sat across from Moose was eating carefully. He stopped and looked at her. "Eat like me," she said. She made exaggerated motions, taking a small forkful of food and placing it carefully in her mouth. Then she looked up at Moose. He tried to follow suit, but he loaded up his fork with more food than he could possibly put in his mouth. "Like this," she said, repeating the motion.

"No," said Moose, and he loaded up another forkful.

"Then eat by yourself!" she said and rose to go.

Moose glanced up at her and greatly modified his forkful. She sat down, and they continued to eat together, with Moose looking first at her fork, then at her face. They were grinning at each other and dining away like old friends. When he finished, he came up to me proudly.

"I have dinnah wid Sawah."

"Yeah," I said, "I know. I saw you."

Moose stood erect and lifted his chin. Then he laughed in that high howl of his that denotes something more than mortal delight.

At five the next morning, I pulled my car out of our driveway and paused for a moment to watch two squirrels fetching acorns from the ground beneath the trees. They moved on silent pads and suddenly disappeared. The birds were taking particular pains not to sing yet, and the aspens stood motionless against the yellowing horizon. The rumble of my car was the only sound in the morning, and I felt I was ripping something beautiful asunder.

I slid the car into camp quietly, relieved to shut off the engine. The quiet closed in around me like a comfortable sweater, and I found myself walking softly through the underbrush to the camp dining room. The quiet brought me within a few steps of a group that Alex was addressing.

"This morning," Alex said, "we're going to take a nature walk. Some of you might want to find out the names of the trees and the birds and the animals that live in our surroundings. Or you might wish to learn the secrets that nature discloses only to those with sharp eyes and the patience to observe. Now, nobody *must* go. It's strictly for those who want to go. Furthermore," he said, "I really want those who don't swim to remain at camp and learn." He looked pointedly at Moose and Tony Brown. "You'll get badges for learning to swim, and I will personally take you on a nature walk so that you won't miss anything."

Moose lit up at the promise of a badge, but Tony reacted much less enthusiastically. At any rate, when the others moved toward their dormitories to get their gear together, Tony and Moose dallied. "I'm real proud of you guys for staying behind for your swimming lessons," Alex said to them. "What I'd like you to do is go to the mess hall, get some milk and some sweet rolls, and then wait until the others clear camp. Laura will meet you there and take you to the swimming pool for your lesson."

We had been trying to get Moose to swim for years, but our enthusiasm had not overcome his fear of water. Moose floated about as easily as a rock, and when Alex volunteered Laura's instruction, I wasn't sure that he knew what he was getting her in for. But then I figured, maybe a part of her participation on the camp staff was to learn, too.

When Moose and Tony went into the mess hall, I approached Alex. "Do you mind if I watch the swimming lessons?"

A hint of a smile seemed to flash behind those thick lenses in Alex's glasses. Something about me was amusing him, but I wasn't much for solving those kinds

of mysteries. "Suit yourself," he said. "I think you'll find
Laura an adequate instructor. But please stay out of sight
so the boys won't be distracted."

I walked to the pool, settled myself unobtrusively a
little way away from it, and waited for the swimming
instructor and her two pupils.

Laura strode down the path gracefully, her hair
blowing over her ears in the morning breeze. She was
small, but wirey, and quite beautiful, with high cheeks
and turned-up nose. Tony towered over her with much
less grace, and Moose bounced along behind him. Tony
hardly seemed to share Moose's excitement; he kicked at
a rock angrily and mumbled, but Laura didn't seem to
notice.

When they reached the edge of the pool, Laura
turned to them and surveyed them thoroughly. Tony
looked at the water as if it were the enemy, and Moose,
forgetting his earlier enthusiasm, was wide-eyed and
fearful. With the slightest suggestion, he would have
turned and fled the scene, happy to have the thing out of
sight and out of mind.

Laura seemed to have completed her strategy-
making and moved toward Moose. She put her
arms around his neck and gave him a big kiss on the
cheek. "Moose, you're very brave to come out here today,
and I want to show you that if you try not to be afraid,
you can learn to swim."

She went to the shallow part of the pool, jumped
into the water and motioned for Moose to follow her. He
sat on the edge, the water up to his knees. Then she took
him by the hands and pulled him all the way in,
apparently oblivious to the fact that he was frightened to
death.

Moose fixed his eyes on Laura's as his body
accustomed itself to the temperature of the water. So far
so good. He was up to his waist in water.

"First," Laura said to Moose, "we want to move in
the water with rhythm. If we move with rhythm we can
learn to use the water as our helper, rather than our
enemy." She put her hands on the side of the pool, then
laid her body out flat in the water and kicked her feet.
Then she asked Moose to do the same. After watching
her, Moose was able to approximate what she was doing.

"When's it my turn?" Tony asked.

Laura turned to Moose and asked him to continue the exercise. Then she pulled herself out of the water and went over to Tony.

"Give me a hug and a kiss like you gave him," Tony said, with great display.

Laura walked up to Tony and put her tiny hand in the middle of his chest. "I think you're all show, no go," she said, and gave him a firm shove. Tony's eyes got big in his head as he incredulously backed up to gain his balance. "Come catch me," she said, and she dashed for the pool. Tony, regaining his balance, if not his composure, raced after her and narrowed the gap considerably until she plunged into the water. Tony screeched to a halt at the water's edge. "Maybe I was right," she said, and splashed water at him. Mustering all his courage, he leaped into the water, and flailed about like a lame duck trying to fly out of a pond. With practically no effort, Laura floated on her back just two feet out of his reach. When she got to the edge of the pool, she jumped up and out and stood there at the edge.

"Hey," she said, "you *do* have the courage; you just lack a little skill. Now come and get me," she said. Tony extracted himself from the pool, and again chased her at full tilt. She jumped into the water and effortlessly stayed out of reach while he put on a great performance of splash and kick, nearly emptying the pool as he did. Again she slid out of the water and onto the edge. While he was panting with near exhaustion, she taught him his first lesson.

"You're trying to fight the water," she said pleasantly. "Now let's see if you can begin to use it to your advantage. You have strong legs, Tony," she said, "learn to use them. Learn to kick them like Moose is learning to do." Tony looked at Moose, who was trying with limited success to duplicate Laura's example. Tony tried, and did fairly well the first time. "Keep it up," Laura said, slapping him on the shoulder.

While Tony practiced his kicking, Laura went back to Moose and jumped in the water beside him. She gave Moose a big hug and said, "You're doing beautifully, Moose. Now let's try to put it together with the movement of your hands." She taught Moose a simple stroke. Over and over, she had Moose repeat the stroke. Now, Moose can't see with his glasses off, but Laura was very close, and he reached out and touched her. "I'm here," she said quietly to Moose, "you're all right." Moose put his arms around her and gave her a big hug, then began practicing again. Laura moved away and went over to Tony.

Tony leaped into the water, and bounced toward her, paddling with his hands to help his speed. "I want you to lie flat, in a dead man's float," Laura said to him. "Push off the bottom with your feet, extend your arms, hold your breath, and float."

Tony ignored her, and made a lunge, reaching for her. Laura saw Tony's intention and sidestepped his grasp. She kicked his feet out from underneath him, grabbed him by the hair, and pulled his face into the water. A moment later she pulled his head out of the water and laughed. "See, you almost did it that time. Now when I ask you to do a dead man's float I mean for you to kick out and lie like a log in the water. Do I need to give you some assistance or can you do it by yourself?"

Without saying a word, Tony kicked off from the bottom of the pool and tried to act like a log.

Laura went over to Moose to see how he was progressing with his paddling. She put a hand on his shoulder. "You're paddling very nicely, Moose," she said. "You're really doing well." Moose looked up and tried to focus his eyes on her. It was not easy without his glasses.

"I like sandwich. Let's go to mess hall. I get dry; use towel. Let's go talk. Let's play chess. Let's go eat. I make my bed. I forget something at home."

Laura looked at him and smiled. "Okay, Moose," she said affectionately, "we'll stop for now. But you're doing a great job. Tomorrow I want you to put it all together."

The next morning, Laura was firm. "I don't want you to learn the pieces and not know the whole thing," she told Moose. "Now I'm going to hold you by the trunks. She flipped him over into the water. "Kick," she insisted, and Moose started kicking. "Now stroke like I showed you," she said, and Moose started moving his hands awkwardly like a windmill. With one hand, she held him up by his trunks, and with the other she helped get his hands in coordination. Soon Moose was managing a distant approximation of swimming. "Excellent,

Moose!'' she said. ''Keep it up.'' Moose looked after her as she moved toward Tony. Laura turned around with a stern look on her face and shook her finger at him. ''I told you to practice,'' she said, and he did.

Laura noticed that Tony's hair was still dry. ''Come on, time to float,'' she said. Tony hemmed and hawed and made lots of excuses.

''We're going to do this by degrees, Tony, and you're going to have your face in the water in a very few minutes.'' She cupped her hand with water in it, and threw it in his eyes. He blinked his eyes and lashed out with both hands. ''It's okay to be afraid of the water,'' she said, ''but you can learn *not* to be.'' Again she filled her hand with water and rubbed it across his forehead. ''See,'' she said, ''that's not so bad.'' She did that again and again, and pretty soon she was taking two handfuls of water and putting it in his face. ''Don't *fight* it, Tony,'' she said, ''*feel* it. It doesn't feel bad, does it? You can handle it. Take a breath, Tony; you can handle it.'' In a few minutes she had Tony standing there, fairly relaxed, while she threw water in his face.

''Now you have to put your face in the water and remain in control of yourself.'' She demonstrated by putting her face in the water after taking an exaggerated breath of air. Tony tried it and got the tip of his nose in the water before he panicked. ''Great,'' she said, ''that's good, do it again.'' When he put his nose in the water, she put her hand on the back of his head and gently immersed his face. He lurched out of the water, as if betrayed. Then he realized what she had done and that he could do it himself. In the next few minutes, he stuck his face in the water many times, emerging with a broad grin and a gleeful ''Look, I did it. I did it!''

Laura then went over to Moose. ''Time for the deep water,'' she said.

At first, Moose was terribly uncoordinated, and it looked as if he were going to drown them both. As they moved about, however, Moose began to get the idea. Then Laura took Moose over to the side of the pool, helped him climb up on the edge, and gave him a big kiss. Moose beamed at her ecstatically. ''Swim,'' he said with a bright smile, ''I swim.''

Laura jumped up and down and clapped her hands. ''You sure did,'' she said, ''you sure did!''

As she continued to work with Moose, Laura used her own body and encouragement as a firm support to which Moose could cling. At the same time, she used Tony's attraction to her as a lure. I was amazed at her success with them.

The lesson ended and Moose and Tony toweled themselves off on their way to the mess hall.

After lunch, Laura called Alex over to the pool with her two pupils. "Who can get across the pool first?" she asked.

I think she helped Moose into the water with a little shove, and he went in with a gigantic splash. He struggled and huffed and paddled and kicked and finally reached the other side. With great effort, he extracted himself from the pool and looked proudly at Laura. She was there with a hug and a squeeze.

Tony, seeing this, was close to follow, and he leaped into the water. Stiffly, he paddled his way across the pool, puffing from the great exertion. "You did a great job, Tony," Laura said, "and as your swimming teacher, I am proud of you."

"I've got to hand it to you, Alex," I said. "You've got the best damn staff I've ever seen."

Behind Alex's glasses, I could see just a hint of amusement. "You like her, too?"

"How could you *not* like her?" I looked at Alex. "What's her name?"

Alex knitted his brows. "I thought you knew." He pulled at his chin. "Lorilei Alexopolus."

"I should have guessed," I said half aloud, "I should have guessed."

"See you tomorrow," he said as I sauntered off to my car.

I came into camp a little earlier the next day, parked the car, and headed for the dormitories. I wanted to see how Alex got them tidied up so quickly each morning.

Moose was just awakening as the radios began to pop off like teapots reaching a boil. His hands poked around tentatively, and he furrowed his brow in a vain effort to bring the world into focus. "Kurt, Kurt," he said urgently, "my glasses!"

The boy in the next bunk handed them to Moose and began making his bed.

But Moose smiled devilishly and trotted off toward the kitchen, unaware that his ponderous belly was protruding beneath his pajama top. Moose stormed into the kitchen area and up to Alex. "Juice," he greeted happily. "Juice. Cereal."

Alex pretended not to hear his request. "Good morning, good morning," Alex said cheerily, "It's good to see you. Is your bed made, and is your personal space clean and tidy?"

Moose stopped short. He blinked at Alex, and his mouth fell open. "Bed made," he said, trying to achieve a tone of conviction, but failing miserably.

Alex smiled. He read the tone more than the words. "Let's go check it then," Alex said.

Alex started to go with Moose to the dormitory, but Moose stopped him at the door. "I'll make it," Moose said.

Alex smiled and came back to the kitchen. He poured me a cup of coffee and then collapsed into his own chair in a pile of arms and legs and elbows and knees. He sipped his coffee and made an exaggerated "Ah!" in appreciation. Moose's response had been a sweet reward.

When Alex mentioned that he was going to have contests for the campers the following day, it suddenly occurred to me that this was an opportunity to switch things around for Moose and his brothers. Moose had spent much of his lifetime in the stands, rooting for his brothers. I couldn't count the times that Moose had watched Eric, Michael, Markel, and Chris, and in more recent years, David, Aaron, and Brett play football, basketball, and baseball games, and compete in track events. Moose was always a dependable and enthusiastic fan of his brothers. Whenever there was a game, Moose asked if he could go and reminded his mother or myself to take him. He cheered for them, win or lose. The fact that they were *there*, participating in an exciting event was sufficient to win Moose's wholehearted approval. He was a loud, clapping, foot-stomping, pop-drinking fan. Sometimes people misunderstood his style, for he would applaud when his brothers dropped a pass as well as when they caught one. But Moose knew their teams and he knew the numbers they wore. He knew when they were on the bench and when they were on the field. From time to time when he was in the stands, he would elbow the person sitting next to him, regardless of who it was, and say, "That's my brother." He knew what the scores were, who had won, and what the individual statistics were of each of the boys. His complete and joyous approval of their every action was simply part of Moose's affection for them.

Therefore, when Alex told me that Moose would participate in the camp events, it seemed to me to be a great opportunity for Moose to be on the receiving end of some applause. I went home that night and told the boys about it.

The next day at the appointed time, Alex began organizing the camp residents into their teams and lining them up for their activities. I arrived in the van, overloaded with boys from the house. We knew the sprints were going to be the first event, so we lined up all along the course. This way we'd be able to cheer Moose each step of the way.

Jackie Arneson captained one team and Tony Brown the other. Each, in turn, picked members for their teams, though Alex was careful to make sure the teams were fairly well-balanced in terms of athletic talent. Moose was on Jackie's team.

We had just gotten comfortably situated when the sprints were announced. Tony and Jackie were the first runners. They got down into a crouch and listened to Alex as he counted, "ready, one . . . two . . . three . . . GO!" The race was close, though Jackie narrowly nipped Tony. That was one point for Jackie's team in the sprints.

At the conclusion of the first four races, the teams were tied at two and two. The last sprint would decide who won the event. For the fifth race, it was Moose against Tillie McMahon.

"Go!" shouted Alex.

Tillie fell at the start, and Moose went over to see if she was all right. Tillie scrambled to regain her balance, and Moose's teammates pointed him in the direction of the finish line. His feet moved so quickly the eye could hardly follow them. Tillie loped along in an uneven and unsteady gait, but her strides were so large that she ate up eight of Moose's steps with one of hers. It was a nip and tuck race as they came to the halfway point, and the boys and I were cheering Moose on as loudly as we could.

"Come on, Moose," Eric said, "dig, dig."

"Come on, you big Puskie," Chris cheered.

"You've got her, Moose, you've got her," Mike and Markel chimed in.

Suddenly, Moose wheeled in the direction of our voices, his face lighting up at the sight of us. He stopped in his tracks, ran over to us, threw his arms out, and embraced first Eric and then each of the other boys in turn.

"Give me a kiss."

"Get back to the track!" Eric shrieked. "She's getting ahead!"

"Moose," Markel yelled, "you haven't finished the race!"

We all hurried him back to where he was supposed to take up the race and pointed him in the direction of the finish line. But Moose was not in a running mood. "You came to see me wun!" he exclaimed, delighted. Then he clapped his hands and jumped up and down at the thought. The immensity of the occasion was not wasted on good ol' Moose.

By this time Jackie Arneson had rushed up, bellowing at Moose at the top of his lungs. "You dumb ninny!" He was pounding on Moose's back. "Finish the race you dummy, we need the point!"

But it was too late. Jackie sighed like a punctured balloon. "You dummy, you made us lose the race."

Eric and the boys were probably disappointed in Moose's performance, but they weren't about to let anyone pick on Moose this way. Eric looked up at Jackie and glared at him. "Who're you calling a dumb ninny?"

Jackie Arneson was probably twice Eric's size, and at least a couple of years older. "I thought blacks were competitive," Jackie said in complete exasperation.

Eric looked from one boy to another. They were all a little exasperated with Moose. Then Eric took a deep breath and sighed. "I guess every person decides for himself what's important," he said. He went over to Moose and hugged him. "You overgrown whale," he said. Moose jumped up and down while the rest of the boys closed ranks around him. They hugged him and slapped him on the back.

While the boys exchanged friendly insults, laughing and embracing each other, Alex stood off to one side, looking pleased.

The events continued and Jackie's team won about as many as they lost. In fact, after eight events, the teams were tied four to four. Now came the tug of war. Five contestants gathered on each side of a big mud puddle, holding a long rope over the mud. Alex signaled the start, and a great deal of tugging ensued.

At first, Tony's team began to edge away from the mud puddle, drawing Jackie's team closer. Moose was the first and closest to the mud puddle, and as he was pulled closer and closer to the mud, his eyes searched for an alternative.

"Come on, Moose," Jackie said. "Pull! Get your mind to it."

Grudgingly, Jackie's team gave ground, and the edges of Moose's boots began to slip into the mud puddle. By this time, Moose was perspiring furiously, and really leaning into the task. In a final display of effort, Moose dug his heels in just as some of the mud trickled into his boots. He let out a shriek of laughter as the cold mud tickled his feet, and his jerks began to shake the rope. Tony's team, hearing and seeing Moose burst out in laughter, began to giggle themselves, and what appeared to be an easy victory began to crumble. As they giggled, their grips loosened and their legs eased. With renewed effort, Moose and Jackie's team pressed their advantage and pulled away from the mud puddle with ever increasing force. Finally, the first member of Tony's team was dragged into the mud. By the time the third member was ankle deep, the team gave up and Moose practically single-handedly pulled the rest of them through the puddle. Jackie's team immediately threw their hands up in a shout of triumph, and the members clapped Moose on the back as if it was entirely his victory.

"Gimme kiss, 'ackie," Moose said. Jackie recoiled, then he shrugged, planted a kiss on Moose's cheek, and cracked him on the back. They all laughed.

Alex was quick to bring out the winners' loot—two cases of soda pop. His strategy soon became clear. The winners uncapped pop for themselves, and realizing there was more than they could possibly drink at one sitting, opened soda for the losers as well.

Moose finished first one bottle of pop, then another. Halfway through a third, he eyed the mud puddle. Suddenly, he leaped to his feet, ran toward the puddle, jumped high into the air, and landed fanny down in the mud, splattering everyone in sight. Moose laughed shrilly and rolled around in the mud until he was thoroughly coated. Seeing this, Jackie followed Moose's example. He took off for the mud with a flying leap and slid clear across the puddle in one dive. Soon all the kids were rolling around in the mud.

I looked over at Alex to see what he thought of this. He sat there, sipping a bottle of orange soda pop and grinning to himself. He nodded at me enthusiastically.

I wondered what I'd do if I were camp director. It seemed a little crazy to play in mud when there was a swimming pool only a few yards away. Finally Alex could resist no longer. He got up and raced toward the mud. He flung himself headlong into the puddle, crashing into Jackie on the other side. They both laughed and began packing mud on the top of each other's heads, leaving me to sit by myself on the embankment.

What the hell, I thought, stripping off my sweater.

After cleaning up from the mud party, the kids decided they wanted to try their hand at making things out of clay. One of Alex's staff was showing them how to use a potter's wheel.

Moose and Tillie McMahon, however, were not particularly interested in the potter's wheel. As a matter of fact, they were preoccupied with each other off to one side of the group. They had some clay between them, and they were taking turns molding odd shapes and showing them to one another. Moose made something that looked to me like a snowman and set it down on the table. He looked at Tillie for her reaction. She clapped her hands and giggled with glee, and Moose leaned across the table and kissed her. Then it was her turn. She made something flat that might have been a maple leaf. Moose stood up, made his body rigid, threw his chin high in the air, and clucked like a chicken. Then he laughed, sat down, and grinned broadly at her. Tillie threw her arms around him and hugged him.

Tony was working on the wheel. I watched as his huge hands attempted to form a small, delicate bowl. Just before he completed his masterpiece, the edges of the clay collapsed. Within a split second, he raised his fist and smashed it, swearing violently.

The instructor looked steadily at Tony and said, "Well, that's one way to rework the clay, but here is another way." She picked the clay up, wedged it on a wire and kneaded it carefully into another ball. She put it back on the wheel and looked at him. "You want to try it again?" She waited patiently as he made up his mind. Slowly, reluctantly, and with great effort, his hands moved toward the clay and began to shape it again.

"What do you think of Tillie and Moose?" I said over his shoulder.

Tony broke into a wide grin. "They're a couple of real lovebirds, ain't they?"

I looked over at Moose. He had fashioned a ring that would fit Tillie's finger and was now putting what resembled a large diamond on top of it. He put it on the "to be fired" table and then came over and tugged my sleeve to show me what he had done. Then he dragged me over to Tillie. "This is Tillie," he said, importantly. "This is Pufessa Oden." Then Moose dismissed me. I waved goodbye to Alex, told him I'd see him in another week, and headed for my car. Professor Oden, I thought to myself. Aren't we getting formal?

Polly and I went to the Y to pick up Moose and Tony. We waited in the parking lot at the appointed time. After about thirty minutes, we saw the van turn into the parking lot and come to a halt in front of the buildings. As soon as it stopped, a roar of human voices exploded from it. The doors flew open as tired bodies tumbled out. Everyone seemed to be talking at once. Tony was with Jackie, and Moose was talking to Tillie.

Tony saw us waiting and got his bags from the van. He looked over at Alex and Laura and started to move toward them. He hesitated, then walked over to Alex and shook his hand. "Thanks," he said to Alex, and for the first time since I'd known him, the steel curtain dropped from his eyes. "Really, man," he said, "I like your camp." He started to say something to Laura, but obviously felt embarrassed. Instead he looked down at the ground. Laura immediately put her arm around Tony and gave him a kiss. Lightly and easily, she stepped back from him.

"You were fun to work with," she said. "You're a good athlete and a fine young man."

Tony's cheeks got darker and he turned his back on

her. "Thanks," he said, without raising his face. "You all helped me a lot."

We waited for a few minutes, anticipating that as soon as Moose saw us he would break away and run to us. Finally, we grew impatient and went to him. He looked at me, and he looked at Polly. Then he turned back to Tillie and continued talking. Other parents showed up and Alex helped them unload suitcases and duffle bags. People began disappearing. Polly and I exchanged glances, partly disappointed that Moose had not shown a great display of affection for us, and yet somewhat amused and proud of his exercised independence.

I stepped forward and took Moose by the shoulder. "Moose, you ready to go home?"

He shook my arm off. "I don't see you," he said. He continued talking to Tillie.

Finally, Tillie's parents arrived to collect her. Seeing their relationship on the verge of ending, Moose looked up at Alex. "Camp is good," he said.

He came over to us then, broke into a broad smile, and embraced his mother and kissed her. Then he hugged and kissed me. He stood there for a moment. "Fat Puskie," he said, finally, "you big fat Puskie."

On the way home we stopped off for dinner. Moose wanted a steak, so we ordered one. With a flourish, Moose picked up the silverware. Slowly and carefully, he ate with his fork and his spoon, his little finger slightly raised.

"I got two girlfriends," Moose said. "I like camp."

Two months later, out of the blue, Moose was bored. We were sitting around the table after breakfast; the boys were playing chess, reading the paper, and wasting some time before they dove into their chores. Moose came up to me.

"Can I have a quarter?" he asked.

"What do you want with a quarter, Moose?"

"I want to go to camp."

CHAPTER ELEVEN

On Moose's nineteenth birthday, the temperature hung around zero. We huddled quietly around the kitchen window, watching the early sun splinter into rainbow columns through the glass.

When Polly and I gave Moose a digital watch, he unwrapped it eagerly and strapped it onto his wrist. He had seen them advertised on television and refused all offers of help or instruction. Moose took off his glasses and examined the dial from a vantage point about two inches from his nose. He pressed the button at its edge and watched as the numbers 12:01:08 flashed before him. Moose grinned and pressed again. In quick succession, the numbers 09, 10, 11, and 12 registered the flying seconds.

Proudly, Moose took his new watch around to each of the boys and demonstrated the magic numerals. Then Moose showed them to me again. He giggled each time the watch responded to his touch.

"You big fat turkey," I said affectionately. "What time is it?"

Moose straightened up with exaggerated dignity, pulled back his sleeve, and cleared his throat. With a flourish, he lifted his glasses and pressed his nose to the glass. "One-two-one-eight-four-six!" Moose broke into his best how-am-I-doing grin.

"I asked you the time, Moose, not the American League batting averages. What do all those numbers mean?"

Moose looked at me soberly. "I tell time," he said, before plowing through the same old numbers routine again.

"You Puskie. That watch is completely useless to you like that. If you come to me in my study at exactly one o'clock, I'll give you a sack of chips."

At exactly one o'clock, there was a knock at my door. "Come in," I said.

There Moose stood, with his glasses in hand, staring at his watch. "Chips," he said.

I reached behind my chair and fingered the crackling paper bag. I looked at the chips, and I looked at him. Then I tossed him the bag. Moose slammed the door, giggling all the way down the hall. "You ringer," I shouted after him, "you big fat ringer."

Snow fell heavily all the next day, so we weren't surprised when Bill Talbot called us and asked for some help clearing his driveway. A neighborhood boy had formerly been under contract to keep the Talbots' driveway and paths cleared, but the boy had moved out of town. Talbot was wondering if any of our boys would like to contract to clear it regularly the rest of the winter. I told Talbot to hang on a minute while I asked Eric.

Eric, however, chose not to make the decision alone. He called in the twins, and they called in Tony and Chris. Pretty soon the room was full of boys, and they arrived at an answer together. The decision was simple: They wanted the contract and the entire group would be responsible for it. Since Eric was into his guitar lesson and didn't want to be disturbed, and since Markel was coaching little league basketball that morning and Michael was playing in a basketball tournament, Chris said he'd take it. So the contract was struck between Talbot and the boys. The only thing I needed to do on this occasion, and I made it clear that I wasn't going to do it all the time, was drive the company over to the Talbots.

I climbed into the van, tooted the horn, and waited impatiently. Out came Moose, followed by Chris. When I got out to help Chris load the snowblower, Moose picked up one end and helped us lift it into the van.

When we arrived at the house, Moose made a beeline for the doorbell. Mrs. Talbot answered the door and Moose announced, "Company here. Pixie, pease." Soon Pixie appeared at the door, and I thought that would be that. I was going to watch Chris only long enough to be sure that he could get the machine operating properly; then I was going to go on about my own business. But by the time Chris started the snowblower, Moose finished his dialogue with Pixie and came down to give Chris directions. With a great deal of arm waving and shouting above the sound of the motor, Moose told Chris what paths he should take. Moose was as serious about his work as a captain of a sail boat in a hurricane.

Pixie observed from the door as Moose rushed about giving verbal and gestural suggestions to Chris. Chris was trying his hardest to ignore Moose's "assistance."

When I came back after an hour, Moose was still giving plenty of directions and was now walking beside Chris to show him exactly where he should go. Moose put one hand on the snowblower handle and looked to see if Pixie was watching.

As Chris finished the job, Moose relinquished his advisory capacity and again moved back to the door to talk to Pixie. He was gesturing wildly to her, apparently explaining how difficult it was to operate the snowblower and how, only through his active guidance, was Chris able to manage the job. Pixie, of course, was duly impressed.

Then Chris went to the door, received his remuneration from Talbot, and stated he would be back with the next snowfall. Talbot nodded at the agreement and waved at me.

When Chris got back to the house, he gave Moose one dollar of the total payment. Moose grinned from ear to ear, probably with pictures of barbecue chips dancing in his head.

At first I was going to ask Chris why he had given a dollar to Moose. The boys had been taught not to give anything away to somebody who hadn't earned it. But when I got to thinking it over, I recalled that they'd also been taught to appreciate effort as much as finished results, and ol' Moose had certainly made an effort.

About a week later, the Minnesota heavens again cascaded snow upon the countryside. Immediately the phone rang, and Moose reached it first. He tried for a moment to maintain a conversation; then hollered for Eric. It was Talbot.

This time the twins went to do the snowblowing. They loaded the snowblower into the van with Moose's verbal and physical assistance.

After Moose had his brief but already traditional conversation with Pixie at the front door, he gave explicit directions to the twins. They struggled together through the task of clearing the driveway and the sidewalks between the house, the barn, and the guesthouse. Pixie waited and watched as Moose told the twins that they should make a wider space for the paths so that people could walk side by side. It seemed like a good suggestion, so the twins began to widen the paths they had already cleared. Finally, Moose intervened completely, took the helm and tore off across the lawn. The twins raced after him, screaming that he was off course.

Suddenly Moose and the snowblower came to a dead stop. A broken lawn-sprinkler lay mangled and detached in the snow. The blower had snapped the sprinkler off neatly.

Moose immediately went to Pixie and pointed out what he had done. "You gotta be careful," he told Pixie. Then he went back to the twins to remind them that one must be careful not to tear up the sprinkler head when snowblowing.

Markel called and suggested that I pick up the nipple and sprinkler head to complete repairs. We repaired the damage in a few extra minutes while Moose explained each move we should be making in his own way.

The twins divided up the payment and laid a dollar on Moose.

By now Moose had been bitten by the gold bug. He'd learned that doing chores converted to cash, and he certainly knew what a little cash converted to.

Coming into my study the next day, he said, "House full wubbish." I looked about me, and had to admit that if my room was any indication, the house certainly was full of rubbish. I started to go back to my work, but Moose pressed the point. "I burn," he suggested.

Normally, the trash collector carried away the garbage, but we also maintained a fifty-five gallon drum behind the barn for excess combustibles we could burn ourselves. Since we didn't burn regularly, that chore was not on our weekly list. And, if I read Moose right, he was putting the bite on me. "Okay, Moose," I said, marveling at his industry, "how much?"

He held up two fingers. "Two dollah," he said, his grin a little uncertain.

"Done." We shook on it and I went back to my work. I thought about Moose and his interest in making money. At nineteen, Moose was becoming practical. I wondered again just how independent Moose would be. If effort counted, he'd make it pretty soon. But effort alone wasn't sufficient for Moose.

I suddenly had second thoughts about Moose burning the rubbish by himself and called for Michael to check on Moose's progress.

I went back to my studies again, but not for long. Polly's scream yanked me out of my thoughts. "Moose! Look at you!"

I tore downstairs three at a time and found Moose standing in the center of the kitchen, ashen. Polly was dancing around him, wringing water on the smoldering holes on his coatsleeves. Moose just stood there, blinking and speechless. His cap was scorched, and I snatched it off and threw it in the sink.

"Moose? Are you all right?"

He opened an innocent, slightly frightened smile at me. "'At's hot!" he said.

"It happened so fast," Michael said. "I couldn't keep him away from the barrel. I thought he was going to jump in!"

The accident might have been serious, but as I looked from Michael to Moose, I had to hold back my laughter. With that wide-eyed expression, Moose resembled a gigantic baby. "No more rubbish burning, Moose," I said. "Okay?"

He looked at me with relief and nodded vigorously.

Soon after the next heavy snow, Eric took his turn at the Talbots'. Moose, of course, was along to help. This time Moose took a couple of packages of corn chips to share with Pixie. She and Moose stood at the door eating chips until Moose's sense of responsibility emerged. He left his chips with Pixie and marched over to Eric. He struggled with Eric to take control of the snowblower, but Eric held firm.

"We don't need another broken sprinkler," Eric explained. "You let me know how I'm doing, and that's all I need from you." So Moose pointed and gestured as he had done in the past, staying half a step in front of Eric.

"Is way, Ewic. Look! Bump!"

On he went until the driveway was clear. Then he went back to Pixie for a few moments. "I buy next time, too," he told Pixie, referring to the chips, and she looked admiringly at him.

During the next two trips to the Talbots' Moose followed the boys' exact footsteps. Finally, Moose told the boys he knew the path that should be taken and begged for permission to push the snowblower for awhile. It was Chris who gave Moose a chance. He walked behind Moose all the way, encouraging him step by step, "Atta boy, Moose, keep it going. Go this way now. Not so fast, Moose, slow down. There's no hurry." Together, they completed the job.

At the end of the day, Moose told Pixie he'd cleared the entire driveway by himself. This was exactly correct, although it didn't quite clarify the role that Chris had played in directing and guiding his every move.

As winter gave way to spring, the contract between Talbot and the boys took on a few extra angles. The snow clearing expanded to planting shrubs, flowers, and vegetables and trimming trees. Through it all, Moose advised and directed the activities whether the workers heard him or not. He learned to mow the same way he learned to snowblow, by following the boys' exact steps. It was inevitable that Moose would eventually insist on mowing the lawn himself.

Again, Chris was the one who gave Moose a chance. He moved behind Moose, chirping out commands and directions that may or may not have been of use to Moose. At any rate, Moose acted as if he didn't hear Chris and moved much on his own initiative. At the end of the day, Moose was given four dollars. The sudden increase opened his eyes wide. Moose knew that four dollars would buy lots of chips.

The following Saturday, when the twins took the mower to the Talbots', the word was out that Moose could mow the lawn by himself. So when Moose asked to do it again, the twins turned him loose. Without realizing that Chris had made Moose's previous attempt successful, the twins left the front yard where Moose was mowing to take care of the garden. Moose began and was doing just fine until Pixie came out.

"Let's see you mow," she said. Moose was happy to oblige, but in his enthusiasm he charged randomly across the lawn. He was making good time until a loud "clang" temporarily slowed him down. The impact jolted Moose and stopped the mower. Worried by the silence, the twins raced in from the back yard to see what had happened.

They found Moose vigorously pushing the mower across the lawn in spite of the fact that the engine was not working. Not knowing what had happened, the twins started the mower again and pointed Moose in the right direction. Everything was functioning in good order, and Moose capably finished his mowing. Afterward, the boys turned on the sprinklers. A geyser of water marked the spot.

This time, the cost of the parts was deducted from Moose's share of the earnings. Moose didn't understand why he received $1.80 rather than $4.00 until I explained that the parts for the sheared sprinkler came to exactly $2.20.

The next Saturday Moose followed the assigned path he had learned very closely, and when Pixie called to him, he kept his eyes on the track, waved her off and shouted at the top of his lungs, "Can't you see I'm busy?" He ignored her until he had finished the entire front lawn. Then he moved to her side to accept the glass of milk and the cookies she offered.

Moose's experience with the Talbot lawn gave him an idea. He asked the boys to teach him to mow our lawn, and he began doing more and more of it each week as he learned the portions. Again, it was a matter of learning exactly where to walk, to avoid the trees, rocks, and other obstructions in his path. But slowly, and very patiently, Moose did learn the proper path, and by mid-summer he was not only mowing the Talbot lawn but ours each week, too.

Moose's freedom from school attendance left him with large amounts of time, and his daily requests for rides to Pixie's began to wear on Polly's patience. Since a bus ran between our house and theirs, Moose thought he might begin to use some of his money for transportation. His brother David thoughtfully applied the lawn-mowing principles to teaching Moose how to catch the bus to and from Pixie's house. One Saturday, David showed Moose where to walk to catch the bus, how to get on, and how to get off. David helped Moose purchase a long-term bus ticket so that he wouldn't have to worry about correct fare each time he rode. By the end of the month, Moose had learned to walk down our driveway and up the street to where the bus stopped. Moose would then get on board, wait for the driver to stamp his ticket, and find a seat. With his eyes fixed to the window of the bus, Moose would wait until he passed a church and two fire hydrants. Then he would pull the chain, getting off just three doors from Pixie's house.

While we were delighted that Moose was increasing his self-reliance, Bill Talbot was not. One day after Moose had made his fifth or sixth visit, the phone rang. Talbot didn't want to talk to the company. He wanted me.

"How are the boys doing?" I asked, searching for his reason for calling me. I hadn't seen him for awhile and couldn't think of why he was calling.

"The boys are doing fine," he said in a restrained tone. "It was something else I wanted to talk to you about. Moose has been coming over fairly frequently," Talbot said.

"Yes," I said, smiling to myself. "He's really learned a lot since he's been out of school."

"I don't want to sound . . . well, I wonder if he should continue to visit Pixie."

That stopped me. Moose and Pixie? I hadn't seen anything wrong with that.

"Look," Talbot said, "I know Pixie is a grown girl. I know she needs friends . . ." There was a long pause. "I don't want to sound like a bigot, but . . ."

It was like being hit in the stomach. I heaved the air out of my lungs, unable to speak.

"You there?"

"Yes," I began. "I didn't realize Moose was bringing any embarrassment on your daughter."

"Now please understand, Chet," he said. "We've known each other now for several years. You know it's not my feelings I'm concerned about."

"I know," I said, "it's what others might say."

Silence. "I guess you've heard that before."

"I'll tell Moose," I said. I struggled with myself. I thought of hanging up. I didn't want him to know how much that hurt me, but I was trying to learn from Moose that it's wiser to let people know how they affect you. I gripped the phone tightly and let the sweat drip down my forearm and off my elbow. "I want you to know, Bill, how disappointed I am. I guess I know how it is for you. But I also know how hurt Moose will be. And Pixie."

Talbot started to say something more, but realized how meaningless it was and we hung up.

For a long time I thought about how I would tell Moose, but I didn't come up with much. "Moose," I began, "I have bad news."

"What's bad news, Daddy?"

"Mr. Talbot doesn't want you to go to Pixie's house anymore."

"Phooey!"

"Yeah, that's a phooey," I agreed.

"Pixie my wife," Moose said flatly.

"I know you like her," I said. "But you can't go to her house if her daddy doesn't want her to see you."

"Phone!" Moose suggested.

"He won't let her talk to you on the phone either, Moose."

Moose stomped around the room. "Shit! I'm mad!"

I walked over to Moose and put my arm around him, but Moose pushed me away and continued his stomping. He reached a corner of the room and poised his nose a few inches from the two walls.

Everyone tried to talk Moose out of his misery that day, but Moose resolutely refused to cheer up. He turned his radio full blast to country western, jammed his thumb in his mouth, and stationed himself in his room.

When Moose didn't show for lunch, I decided to approach him again. Moose's room was strangely silent. And empty.

One of the boys thought he remembered seeing Moose board the bus, so I called Talbot.

"Pixie's gone, too," Talbot said. "I'll call you if I find out anything."

I piled the boys into the van and we set out, slowly tracing the bus route across town, while Polly kept close to the phone at home. When we reached the downtown section, the boys fanned out to search.

We found Moose and Pixie in an ice cream parlor, drowning their sorrows in strawberry sodas.

"Moose! You big turkey, we're all worried about you."

Moose pretended not to see me. He rose from the booth and headed for the bathroom. After a few minutes, he emerged and returned to his seat beside Pixie. I was trying to decide how to persuade him to come with us when one of the boys suggested I call Talbot. Bill agreed to come to the store and talk with Pixie.

He flew in minutes later, flushed and excited. "Pixie," he said, "you must come home with me right now."

Pixie blew a few bubbles with her straw and remained in her seat. At least Pixie would have been a little easier to move physically than Moose, I thought, but Bill Talbot didn't seem to like the idea any better than I did.

"I'll tell you one thing," I said. "I'm not going to carry them out of here."

Talbot pondered the situation for several minutes.

"Okay," he said finally. "I can see how much this friendship means. Moose, you can see Pixie once a week. For an hour."

Moose looked about the restaurant as if he had all afternoon.

"Maybe twice," Talbot softened.

Moose smiled, Pixie smiled, and we all went home.

* * *

In the middle of July, Cadacious Alexopolus called. He didn't bother to mince words. He explained that his summer camp had become one for mentally retarded teenagers, a dream of his, and that he needed a retarded counselor to live in the residence units with the other kids. He remembered that Moose had enjoyed himself at camp before and had managed to stay out of trouble. Would Moose like to come and help out for two weeks?

I thought Moose would be delighted. When I asked him, he thought it over with furrowed brow, like a man about to make a financial plunge into the stock market. Then Moose looked at me, took off his glasses for a moment, and started counting on his fingers. "Ten dollahs," he said after some consideration, "for ten dollahs."

I didn't believe my ears. Was my Moose proposing that he charge ten dollars for his counseling services?

I didn't know whether to be pleased that he considered his own services worthwhile, or displeased that he charged so little for them. I shrugged. It really wasn't my business what he charged, so I passed his request on to Alex.

Alex was delighted that Moose would charge ten dollars and immediately consented to the fee.

Moose packed his own duffle bag full of sandwiches, corn chips, a bunch of candy bars, hot dogs, apples, and a good deal of Earl, Terry, and Mila's drawings, papers, and homework. I surreptitiously contributed some clothing and a sleeping bag.

On the way to the camp, Moose explained all of the activities that would happen there. He mentioned the swimming pool and how cold it was, the track events (in which physical stamina was emphasized), and the fact that you had to make your bed before you ate breakfast. Certainly he remembered the rules and seemed to be a promising counselor.

Moose called from camp each night to give us brief reports. The first day, he told us there were seven girls and five boys at camp and from his voice I rather suspected he liked the odds in his favor. Moose specified that Brenda was going to be his wife, and Lynn, a counselor, was going to be his wife, too. I asked about Pixie. "She my wife, too!"

Then he asked me to bring a radio out for him so he could listen to country western. "I pay for batteries," said Moose. He was really getting a commercial head on his shoulders.

The third night Moose called, he said he was going to take the bus home the next morning if I didn't come pick him up. Knowing better than to challenge Moose, I showed up in the morning with the van. Moose had his bags packed and was ready to go home. When I asked him why, he said that the Talbot lawn needed mowing and that this was his day to do it. Moose accepted no compromise, so I took him home and let him do his duty with the Talbot lawn. He spent an hour with Pixie, telling her about his new camp job, then explained that he had to get back and finish his two weeks there. The following week was the same story: Moose came home to do the Talbots' lawn, visited briefly with Pixie, and returned to his "new job."

Moose was really beginning to assume some adult responsibilities, and I was proud of him. I wondered if his "wives" had awakened this sense of obligation.

When Moose came home, he showed off pictures of his "wives," pointing out that they all liked him very much. Many of the residents in the unit had cried because they were homesick, Moose said, and he demonstrated to me how he was able to comfort them by putting his arms around them and patting them on the back.

Alex had made a wise choice in his selection of Moose as a counselor, for Moose had helped each of the residents adjust to what was probably their first experience away from home.

The final mark of Moose's independence came when he decided to take Pixie out on a date, using the money he had earned during the summer.

"I take Pixie. See dah monstah. We eat. Ride bus."

Once I convinced myself this was possible, I called the boys together and presented Moose's plan to them. They decided to take on the task of helping Moose organize and carry out his date.

Chris's job was to get Moose and Pixie safely on the bus and off again at the right stop. Together they went through all the steps until Moose knew what to do.

Markel and Michael decided to train Moose to order and pay for dinner. They first considered ordering the whole dinner in advance so that all Moose and Pixie would have to do would be to show up and eat. They both agreed, however, that this was taking all the prerogatives that Moose wanted out of his control. Instead, they went to the restaurant and showed Moose what could be ordered, indicating the different prices and letting him choose himself. They couldn't account for Pixie's tastes in advance, but Moose said Pixie would order whatever he ordered, anyway. Then they tried to teach Moose how to count the money. It was simple enough to figure out the number of dollars. It was the cents that didn't make sense to Moose. The twins finally decided that Moose would give the cashier one dollar more than what was asked for and wait for the change.

Eric took on the task of showing Moose how to dress himself in his best clothes so that they matched. He offered suggestions in a way that made them seem to be Moose's ideas in the first place. Eric also suggested a good monster movie.

If there was anything that Moose would not allow, it would be somebody tagging along just to take care of him. But Eric told Moose he wanted to see the movie for his own benefit, although I had never known Eric to be at all interested in monster movies. Of course, if something went wrong on the date, then Moose would be happy that Eric was there.

On the appointed day, Moose headed out for the bus stop, and Chris set out after him. Suddenly, Chris realized that this was *not* a dry run, and he stopped short. He watched Moose for a long time, wondering whether or not Moose would remember what they'd practiced. Of course he did.

Eric and a friend sat in a car across the street from the bus stop. The motor just happened to be running, and the car just happened to be pointed in the same direction as the bus. Moose pulled his coupon out of his pocket and fingered it, waiting. When the bus came, Moose stepped on board, smiling with confidence. As the bus pulled out, so did Eric and his friend.

Although the exact events are not entirely clear, I managed to piece the evening together from the boys' description. Apparently, Moose got off at the right bus stop, but stopped at a neighbor's garden to collect four red roses instead of going directly to Pixie's. Bill Talbot learned this from the neighbor, a man who felt strongly about his roses.

Moose rang the bell, and when Mrs. Talbot showed up, demanded a kiss before he would enter the house. Mrs. Talbot, having a Down's syndrome child of her own, understood Moose clearly. She gave him a kiss with a hug and ushered him in. Moose and Pixie got on the bus without event and headed toward town, Eric and his friend following at a discreet distance.

After the movie, Moose invited Eric and his friend to join him and Pixie at the restaurant. Moose wanted to treat them all to hamburgers, but with a little reminder from Eric, he remembered that his money wouldn't go that far, so Eric and his friend sipped Cokes while waiting for Moose and his date to complete their evening on the town.

When Moose came home, both Polly and I were still up. As we heard him clumping up the driveway, Polly heaved a great sigh of relief.

Moose came inside, obviously pleased with himself, and I asked him how he enjoyed the movie. He threw his arms over his head, made claws out of his hands, and gurgled a terrible noise.

"Dracula sounds to be in the best of form," I said, and we both laughed. Moose added that the hamburgers were excellent, that the french fries were hot, and that they had had all the salt and ketchup they wanted.

"You can hardly knock that," I said.

CHAPTER TWELVE

By the time Moose was twenty, Earl, Mila, and Terry had completed their education and begun careers. They had married and made their own homes. Their visits were happy occasions, and as they made major decisions in their lives, the telephone lines sung with our messages.

We've encouraged our children to leave home whenever they feel ready. But it's hard to stop being a parent. Watching children break the last controlling bonds and go out on their own can be painful. But it's a pain combined with joy.

With Moose, being a parent goes beyond preparing a child for an independent life. After Moose finished school, we had to do a lot of thinking about his development as an adult. Moose had learned to fix himself simple meals. He did his own laundry, and of course he recognized Frankenstein or Dracula reruns in the newspapers. But we had to wonder how far his development as an independent adult would go. What were his limits? What could we realistically expect of him, and where should we draw the line?

Because Moose liked to drive our little garden tractor, we let him till soil and cut weeds when one of the boys was home to direct him. Moose did a good job, because he is very careful and asks questions when he isn't quite sure of himself. Polly and I let him back the van out of the garage and put the cars away at night. I've let him drive my car on our dirt roads when I've been with him, and he handles the machine well at slow speeds. But he hasn't asked to get a driver's license yet. I don't know what I'll say when he does. I'm sure he can't read well enough to get a license anyway.

I still don't know how financially self-sufficient Moose will become. He first surprised me by pouting when he *didn't* have chores, and next when he did them well. When Moose began "helping" the boys with the Talbot contract I had been surprised as well as impressed. Then, when Moose began contracting around our house for jobs, I was pleased by this positive development. He even began saving a little money.

But I wondered, How far can he go? Is it reasonable to expect him to be able to take work in a "sheltered" workshop? How realistic is it to even consider that he might be able to work at a real job?

Moose had been going on regular dates with Pixie. Their activities were pretty much limited to seeing monster movies, visiting public places in the Twin Cities, especially the zoo, and eating out in a few selected restaurants. But it was apparent that their relationship was special to them. This raised other questions in my mind. Was there going to come a time when Moose might want to move in with her . . . or have her move in with him? Was Moose going to father children? With my older children, such thoughts weren't much of a problem. Those choices were up to them. But what about Moose? How far was Moose from being a full-fledged adult?

My concerns were stoked by a telephone call from Bill Talbot. Talbot had been appointed Chairman of the Governor's Commission for the Employment of the Handicapped. Among the state employees influenced by Bill's hiring policies were the sanitary engineers, the people who swept the halls, cleaned out the wash basins, and disposed of the trash.

Bill Talbot had seen Moose help with the snowblowing and lawn-mowing around his place, and he recognized that Moose could learn simple tasks although rather slowly. Then, when he heard about Moose's counseling experience from Alex, Bill decided to begin an experiment.

Bill called me to offer Moose a job as assistant sanitary engineer in a state building near the capitol. I asked Bill if he could give me forty-eight hours to think it over. Then I decided that since Bill was offering the job to Moose and not to me, I should let Moose decide.

Moose took to the idea right away. When he said the words "Assistant Sani-gineer," he stopped short in his tracks, threw back his shoulders, lifted his chin high, and saluted as if the inspector general were walking by. Moose was excited about the possibilities of earning a real salary and began rehearsing his role. He took possession of all the brooms, mops, and scrub rags in the house, the wax for the floors, the ammonia for the windows, and the cleanser for the basins. The house took on a freshly-buffed sheen.

The only drawback was that Moose expected his salary to begin at home. After Moose finished vacuuming the floors and the furniture, he came to me and demanded a dollar. He also demanded a dollar for washing the windows and another for waxing the floor. When I told him I had not hired him as a "sani-gineer" for our house, he stomped off in a rage. Then from a distance of about ten feet, Moose turned around, shook his finger, and gave me a terrible chewing out.

The boys were able to teach Moose the fundamentals of housekeeping, but they had their difficulties, too. Moose, with his new status, suddenly began limiting the freedom of everyone in the household. If one of us went to open a door and didn't wipe the doorknob after we used it, Moose would come rushing over and scold us. I could not get up early in the morning and shave without receiving a mini-lecture on wiping the mirror clean after I bumped it with a soapy thumb. Everyone in the household received explicit instructions on polishing the water controls in the shower. Ashtrays were redefined as clean receptacles for the very temporary deposit of ashes.

One night at dinner, Moose leaped up from the table and hurried over to take my plate into the kitchen.

"Hold on," I said, "I'm not finished!"

"I do dishes now, vacuum stairs," he said in a grumpy voice.

I grabbed Moose by the arm. "Hey easy, fella," I replied. "Don't you know the sanitary engineers don't touch dirty plates?"

Moose thought I was giving him a dodge, and he persisted. He put his thumb and forefinger on my plate and began to edge it across the table. I was still trying to get the last of the meat and potatoes onto a fork. "Goddamn it, Moose," I exploded, "get your big sani-engineering mitts off my plate!" Moose scowled at me and I scowled back. "The union of assistant sani-gineers are going to hear about you touching people's dinners," I thundered at him, "and they're going to be pretty sore." That got Moose's attention and he loosened his grip. "A sani-gineer has plenty to do keeping floors clean, banisters polished, and windows and mirrors sparkling, and when he's done with all that, he can wash and polish his father's car."

With that Moose's eyes got wide. He didn't realize that automobiles were part of his assignment. He suddenly lost interest in the dinner table and disappeared from the room. Pretty soon I could hear the dull knocking of the water pipe in the basement and the splashing of water in the garage. At least tomorrow I'll have a clean car, I smiled to myself. But I'll probably have to pump a flood out of the garage before I can drive to work.

Arrangements were made for Moose to take the job. Given a liberal period for training, the job was not at all beyond Moose's ability. He was responsible for a single floor in the State Administrative Building, cleaning the floors, emptying the trash containers into a large bin and carrying the bin to the incinerator, cleaning out the restrooms, and vacuuming the offices. The cleaning equipment was not that different from those he had used at home. The brooms were wider, the mops larger, and the vacuum more powerful, but they served essentially the same purposes, and Moose was familiar with each, so training Moose was relatively simple for his brothers.

It was on Friday, the day for mopping, that Moose encountered his first problem. Eric was with him and accepted the blame for the minor mishap.

Moose had filled a bucket with hot water and cleanser and begun mopping the hallway. He was concentrating deeply and failed to notice a door open just off the hallway and a man appear. Moose thrust the mop in the bucket, splashing water profusely over the side and onto the pantlegs, socks, and shoes of Assistant Attorney General Kelly.

Oblivious to what he had done, Moose sloshed the mop from side to side, swabbing Kelly's shoes in the process. Moose had been well-schooled in mopping, and his mop flew from wall to wall, slopping hot suds and. dirty water halfway up to the ceiling.

Kelly stood in the doorway, wringing the water out of his suit and eyeing Moose incredulously. Eric, meanwhile, ran around Kelly, trying to gain his attention and apologize.

At that moment, Attorney Gallagher came out of his office and observed Eric trying to communicate to Kelly. Gallagher was only peripherally aware of Moose, who was in the background swabbing the decks like a sailor.

Gallagher tried with partial success to choke back his laughter. He approached Kelly and slapped him on the back. "Another one of those days?" he said.

Eric interrupted, "Sir, I'm terribly sorry. . . ."

"Who turned that fool loose in here?" Kelly blurted, his complexion reddening.

Again Eric tried to explain. "My brother's new on the job and . . . well, er, I'm teaching him."

"Look at this; just look at this," Kelly said with a sweep of his hands, "and I'm due in court in five minutes."

Gallagher's expression was still amused. "I hope you wore your drip-dry suit." Then Gallagher looked at Moose. "Don't you think he's a little long on enthusiasm?"

By this time Moose had realized that something was wrong. He walked up to Eric, staring, his mop in hand.

Kelly sighed and looked from Eric to Moose. "You're the new employee?"

Eric stepped forward. "This is my brother, Wayne. . . ."

"I'm Moose," Moose said at the same time.

"He's just been brought on as an assistant sanitary engineer," Eric said. "I'm helping him break into the job. I'm terribly sorry this happened."

Kelly looked at Gallagher. "Talbot. This has got to be Talbot's work." Satisfied that he'd found the culprit of his disaster, Kelly's mood changed. "The pants will dry," he acknowledged. "What was that name again?"

"Moose," Moose said emphatically.

"Go easy, Moose," Kelly said. He patted Moose on the back and took off down the hall.

Gallagher lingered for a few moments, watching Eric's interaction with Moose.

"What are you supposed to be doing now?" Eric asked Moose.

Moose looked down at the mop in his hands. He broke into a wide smile. "Oh, ya, get dirty water off floor. Wring out mop. Dump water out."

"You got it," Eric said happily. Moose took off down the hall, swinging his mop with a little less enthusiasm than before, though still making it semi-dangerous to walk.

Gallagher was sufficiently impressed. "I really got to hand it to you," he said, "your brother seems to be catching on."

Later in the week, Moose met Attorney Montag, a man who showed far less tolerance for Moose's efforts to learn his new job.

Eric had just shown Moose how to empty the wastebaskets into the larger bin on wheels. As Moose dutifully emptied wastebaskets from all the offices, Eric, satisfied that Moose knew what to do, sat down to read a magazine. Moose emerged from the last office, his bin piled high with crumpled papers and miscellaneous trash.

Eric jumped to his feet. "Now where do you take that stuff?"

Moose pushed the bin toward the elevators. Eric followed close behind, willing to let him make a small mistake but not a large one. Down the elevator to the basement Moose pushed the bin, with Eric in close pursuit. When the elevator got to the basement, Moose heaved the bin out of the elevator towards the incinerator. There he emptied the papers into a large compartment, closed the door, and pulled the lever that forced the papers into the combustion chamber. Eric was becoming more confident all the time of Moose's ability to handle the job. It wasn't until they got back up into the lawyers' offices, that Eric's new-found confidence was shaken.

Moose knew, upon question, that his next job was to dust the furniture in the offices. But before he even got through the first door, Attorney Montag walked out and confronted him. "Did you empty my wastebasket?" Montag demanded harshly.

It suddenly struck Eric that he'd failed to teach Moose how to respond in a situation like this. When someone, anyone, approached Moose that aggressively, Moose was just as likely to turn on his heel and walk out of the building as he was to stay there. Eric rushed over to Moose's side and whispered into his ear, "Hang in there, Moose. Answer him politely."

Moose looked at Montag with a blank expression while Eric nudged him from behind. Eric was sure the instructions had sunk in and that Moose only needed the proper prodding. Moose, however, stuck his thumb in his mouth and began sucking furiously.

"Yes, sir; he emptied the wastebaskets. He's new on the job," Eric explained, running all of the words together in his hurry to get them out.

Montag looked from Moose to Eric and then back to Moose. "What the hell's going on? Is *this* our new janitor?"

That did it. Moose stomped his foot and shouted directly into Montag's face, "Not janitor! Assistant sani-gineer!" With that, Moose paced around Montag, staring in his ears and at the back of his head.

Montag scowled deeply. "An important contract has just disappeared from my office," he said. "Where's the rubbish? I want you to go through it and find that contract immediately."

Moose stood still now, directly in front of Montag. "In the 'cinerator," Moose said proudly.

Again Eric attempted to explain. "We just finished emptying the trash and putting it in the incinerator as we were instructed."

"This is terrible," Montag boomed. "You burned up an important contract! This is going to cost my department a lot of money, time, and trouble."

"I'm terribly sorry," Eric said, "but we were instructed to empty the trash cans."

Montag leaned threateningly toward Eric. "It wasn't in the damn trash can," Montag shouted. "It was on my desk! You must have taken it off."

Eric looked uneasily at Moose, uncertain about what exactly had taken place in each of the offices. But he was loyal to Moose. "Moose doesn't make that kind of mistake," Eric said evenly. "It must be somewhere if you didn't put it in the trash can, because Moose does *exactly as he is told*."

By this time, Montag's voice had reached storm level. "Don't tell me where my documents are! The contract was on my desk five minutes before you imbeciles went rushing into the offices, throwing away everything you could lay your hands on!"

Eric wilted under Montag's volley but summoned his courage to offer shakily, "We'll be happy to help you look for it."

Montag didn't even hear Eric. He picked up the telephone and called Bill Talbot, demanding that Talbot come down immediately. In a few moments, Talbot eased in and asked Montag what was on his mind.

"These incompetents," Montag began, "have blundered into my office and thrown away a very important contract that was on my desk. To make matters worse," Montag bellowed, "it has already been incinerated!"

Bill Talbot went up to Moose and put an arm around him. "How's it going, boys?" he said. He waited until Montag had cooled down, then turned around. "Okay," he said, "what's the story?"

Eric eyed Montag uneasily. "Well, Moose went into the offices and emptied out the wastebaskets. We took the trash down and put it in the incinerator. Then this gentleman said a document was missing off his desk."

"What they forgot to say is that they took the contract off my desk and burned it with the trash!" Montag's color and voice were rising again.

Talbot scratched his head and turned back to Eric, "Are you sure you didn't throw away the document?"

"Moose usually does exactly what he's told," Eric said, trying to be as truthful as he could, "and I told him not to touch anything on desks or chairs or anyplace else. Just the wastebaskets."

Talbot stood for a moment, apparently reviewing what he knew of Moose. He may have wondered briefly if his experiment was blowing up in his face. Then he turned to Montag. "Have you checked with the secretaries?"

Montag looked impatiently at Talbot. Then he disappeared around the corner. In a few moments he returned. "They haven't seen a damn thing, just as I suspected!"

Finally, Moose opened his mouth to speak. "You tell Pixie I'm working?" he asked Talbot.

"Sure I'll tell her you're working. She'll be proud

of you." Then Talbot asked gently, "Are you *sure* you didn't touch anything on anybody's desk?"

Moose lowered his eyes. "Well," he said, with a voice to match his downcast expression, "matches! I took matches. Dangerous to burn the place." Then Moose began emptying his pockets. He had collected about four dozen books of matches from the tops of desks. "Dangerous," Moose said, "naughty to leave matches laying."

Talbot concealed a smile. "Oh, so now you're the fire marshal, too?" he teased. "It's okay, Moose. You can leave the matches on the lawyers' desks. They can handle them."

Moose glared at Mr. Talbot. "Naughty!"

"Maybe you're right, Moose," Mr. Talbot said, "but you leave them on the desks."

Then Talbot turned to Montag. "You know, Reuben," he said, "this isn't the first document you've misplaced." Talbot began to move slowly toward Montag's office. "You suppose we could have a look around?"

"You won't find it," Montag said. He followed Talbot begrudgingly into his office. Talbot stepped inside. The top of the desk was clear, and the file cabinet and book cases were devoid of loose papers. The wastebasket was clean as a whistle.

"See?" Montag said defiantly.

Talbot stood in the center of the room, deliberating. Then he stepped forward to the desk and pulled out the extra board immediately under the desk top. There, on top, was the contract. Talbot held it up for Montag to see. "Is this your missing document?"

Montag took it with a scowl. Turning to Moose, he asked churlishly, "Dammit! Did you take that contract off my desk and stick it in my drawer?"

Moose reached inside his pocket and pulled out two books of matches. "Sorry," Moose said, laying the matches on Montag's desk.

As Talbot, Eric, and Moose were leaving, Talbot patted Moose on the back. "Remember, just the rubbish in the wastebasket," he reminded Moose.

Eric looked at Moose. "Well now," he said, "what's your next task?"

* * *

Payday was a special event for Moose. He carried the deposit slip in his wallet and showed it to everyone he knew.

On the day after payday, Moose disappeared from the house. We were all so preoccupied that we didn't notice for quite a while.

Moose had taken the bus to Pixie's house, knocked on the door and asked if Pixie could go to the movies. Mr. Talbot had no objections, and he sent Pixie and Moose off to the movies together. So far so good.

When Moose got to the theater box office, he went up to the window as usual. "How many tickets do you want?" the cashier asked. Moose held up two fingers. Then he proudly extracted the wallet from his pocket, pulled out the deposit slip, and passed it to her.

The cashier didn't know quite what to do. She pushed it back to him. "That's not money," she said.

"That money from my job," Moose protested. "I buy two tickets."

The cashier tried to explain that she could not accept deposit slips.

Suddenly Moose felt that he had been betrayed. "That damn gov'ment!" he shouted.

The cashier, sensing disaster, called for the manager, who called me.

Trying to explain deposits and withdrawals to Moose was no easy task, and I realized that we still had a way to go in training Moose how to deal with the outside world.

Yet, there were even more pressing issues to face. The first arose when Moose asked for his own place to live.

Polly and I talked about it a long time. Actually both of us were very much encouraged by Moose's desire for his own home. Not that we were trying to get rid of him; we always considered it important for Moose to be able to live as independently as he could, although we realized he would always depend on us for some things.

What we weren't sure of was whether Moose could manage in an apartment or home some distance from us. Would he understand things like rent payments? Moose was used to having a large family around. Wouldn't he be lonely?

We have eleven acres on our property, with plenty of room for another house. What we finally decided was that by building on our property, Moose could have his own house and still be close enough for us to help him. We could check to see if it was kept clean, to see that it was heated properly, and to make sure there were no fire hazards. We could fix the faucets and keep the stove and refrigerator working.

We told Moose that we would be willing to build another, smaller house on the property for him, and we suggested that he use some of his earnings each month to share the expense. Moose considered our proposition for a time. About five minutes. He liked the idea.

We gave Moose some magazines on home-building, inviting him to look at the pictures and pick out those he liked. We thought this was one way of finding out whether or not he was really interested in his own home.

Several days later, Moose showed me a magazine picture of newlyweds standing in front of a small house. "Husband and wife in house," Moose said. Then he pointed out our window to a group of birch trees behind the barn. "Pixie and I there," he said. "When we start?" So the second critical issue was raised. Moose wanted to share his house with Pixie.

Polly and I decided we'd better talk this over with the Talbots. We didn't know whether Pixie had mentioned marrying Moose to them or not, or whether they would approve.

"You know," I began, "Moose and Pixie have been seeing each other now for five years." I thought my comment was vague enough to begin a discussion rather than a panic.

"How is he doing at work?" Polly asked Talbot.

Talbot pulled his pipe out of his pocket. "We're happy with the program," he said in a professional tone. "Moose is one of our successes." Puff. "Not all a bed of roses, of course." Puff, puff. "But successful."

"Well," I said, after a pause, "I guess this won't be a surprise to you, but . . . Moose is talking about marrying Pixie."

Bill took his pipe out of his mouth and looked to see if it was still burning.

"We're not surprised. Pixie has mentioned it, too, but would that be legal?" Mrs. Talbot wondered.

"They *are* people," Bill reminded her. "But what if we don't permit them to?" Polly and I had been struggling with the same question all week.

"Remember what happened when they felt their relationship was about to be broken up before?" I asked.

"Yeah," Talbot acknowledged. "Don't really know if we could stop them."

"Suppose they do get married," Mrs. Talbot said. "Could they have children?"

"Well, I've been doing a lot of reading about that," I said. "Moose doesn't really have a strong sex drive. Moose and Pixie would probably be companions, not lovers."

"What have you observed when you've seen Pixie and Moose together?" Polly asked gently.

"Well, they're good friends. And they're very affectionate with one another. But not really in a sexual way. . . ." said Mrs. Talbot. Bill puffed and nodded his agreement.

Talbot removed his pipe. "I don't mean to get ahead of things," he said, "but we think a child would be too much for Pixie and Moose to handle anyway. I don't think children would be a good idea. She really struggles to fix her own meals and do the laundry. It takes a lot of effort for her to do her share of the housework. She insists on it and struggles hard just to keep up each day. She couldn't manage that and a child, too, to say nothing of the difficulties in parenting."

"The chances of Moose becoming a father are very remote," I said. "In fact, there has been no documented case of a Down's syndrome male fathering a child. Apparently about half of Down's females can have children, though."

"Sterilization is a possibility," said Talbot.

"That would have to be considered even if they didn't marry," added Mrs. Talbot.

We all agreed that there were a lot of things to think about.

After about a week, the Talbots invited us over for dinner with Pixie and Moose. We ate on the porch, enjoying the sunset and the warm air. Moose and Pixie left to play Ping-Pong and we again raised the subject of their marriage.

"We've been thinking," Bill said. "It's been a long struggle for Pixie. She doesn't have a lot of friends outside her school."

I nodded, thinking Moose was different in that respect.

"A close friend shouldn't be denied someone," Bill said finally. "We've been making decisions for Pixie for a long time, but we'd like her to have . . . some choice."

Polly smiled understandingly. "That's a difficult thing to discover after many years, but I agree. I think we all have to accept that."

"But I definitely don't want them to have children." Bill quickly added. "At one time I might have been opposed to Pixie marrying a black person," Talbot suddenly said. "But that's really not the problem here at all. It's Pixie marrying *anybody*."

"Moose!" I called out. Moose walked in with his Ping-Pong paddle.

"Who is my wife, Moose?"

"Mommy."

"Who is your wife?"

Moose took Pixie's hand and stood stiffly, as if he were facing a minister. "Pixie!" he exclaimed, hugging her suddenly.

"Moose, what are you going to do for the rest of your life?"

Moose scowled at the concept of future. He understood "now" and even "a couple of hours," but "later" was a toughie and the "rest of your life" was a real struggle. He surprised me by saying with certainty, "Work! And love Pixie!"

Later that night I lay awake thinking about Pixie and Moose. There was no doubt in my mind that they loved each other and that they were good companions for each other.

I wondered if they could manage a household. Could they plan a healthy diet and prepare it? How would they manage their personal finances, trips to the grocery store, utility bills? Would they know when to ask for help before getting into serious trouble? The questions were overwhelming, and I didn't know which ones were legitimate and which ones were imagined worries, the worries of a father who was about to lose his son. No, I mean gain a daughter.

* * *

Today is pretty, spring-like, with buds shooting on the branches of the trees. A new day for us all.

This morning we had the usual panic in the downstairs bathroom as our houseful of boys rushed to prepare for school.

Moose wasted no time. He was already upstairs eating his breakfast and reaching into his pocket to be sure he had his bus coupon handy when I walked in. I saw him peek out of the corner of his eye to see what Polly was putting into his lunch. I knew he was anxious to be gone, but he took a moment to give Polly a big kiss and a pat on the back.

"You big fat cow," I teased. "Give me a kiss, too."

I heard the chorus of boys' voices wishing him a happy day and the door slam. Since Moose has been working we expect this ritual each morning. Moose is serious about getting to work on time, about his responsibilities there.

I wonder if he is serious about marrying Pixie, if he understands what marriage means. I wonder if Polly and I will know when to advise him and when to back off.

But hell, why am I going on like this? We've faced other problems before, and I should have learned by now you don't lick them all at once. Moose's future will happen just like his past—first one day and then another and another.

The bus must be coming. I can see Moose dancing up and down in anticipation.

Right now I guess I'm sure of one thing, and one thing only—Moose will make it to work on time today . . . tomorrow? We'll see.

ABOUT THE AUTHORS

Scott MacDonald has worked with people to foster their personal growth since his college days. Working with chronic mental patients, Peace Corps Volunteers, Job Corps persons, delinquents, members of ethnic minorities, and college students has provided opportunities for him to help others in and out of public institutions and to learn from those persons. Scott met Moose as a personal friend seven years ago, but it was only after giving a workshop on mainstreaming in Little Rock, Arkansas that the idea to write *Moose* was born. The participants in that workshop urged that the story of Moose be shared. The project seemed to be a way to inform people who are struggling with the problem of mainstreaming the handicapped into schools and society.

Chester Oden has been an advocate for youth, unofficially, for nearly his entire adult life. With Moose and those like Moose as his impetus, Chet realized that he was more concerned with the minds of people than with their bodies. So he discontinued his medical work and took up psychology and special education. Through Project Discovery, he helped five inner-city St. Paul schools band together to provide meaningful education for youth of all ethnic groups. Chet has helped corrections institutions become more humanely "corrective"; he has influenced schools to expand opportunities for pupils and teachers; and he has served as philosophical conscience as well as psychological consultant for minority groups within the Hennepin County Mental Health Agency. He currently works with group homes to increase the options of foster youth and teaches in the now emerging area of Human Relations at the University of Minnesota.